VAMPIRES

Published in the United States and its territories and Canada by

HAMMOND

HAMMOND WORLD ATLAS CORPORATION
Part of the Langenscheidt Publishing Group
36-36 33rd Street, Long Island City, NY 11106

EXECUTIVE EDITOR: Nel Yomtov
ASSISTANT EDITOR: Kevin Somers

Produced for Hammond World Atlas Corporation by

MOSELEY ROAD INC.
129 MAIN STREET
IRVINGTON, NY 10533
WWW.MOSELEYROAD.COM

MOSELEY ROAD INC.
PUBLISHER Sean Moore
ART DIRECTORS Brian MacMullen, Gus Yoo
EDITORIAL DIRECTOR Lisa Purcell

DESIGNERS Lisa Purcell, Amy Pierce
PHOTO RESEARCHER Ben DeWalt
PRODUCTION DESIGNER H. Hwaim Lee
CARTOGRAPHY Neil Dvorak
EDITORIAL ASSISTANTS Rachael Lanicci, Natalie Rivera

COVER DESIGN Linda Kosarin

Printed and bound in Canada

ISBN-13: 978-0841-611009

HAMMOND UNDERCOVER™

VAMPIRES

DAWN MARTIN

HAMMOND World Atlas
Part of the Langenscheidt Publishing Group

Contents

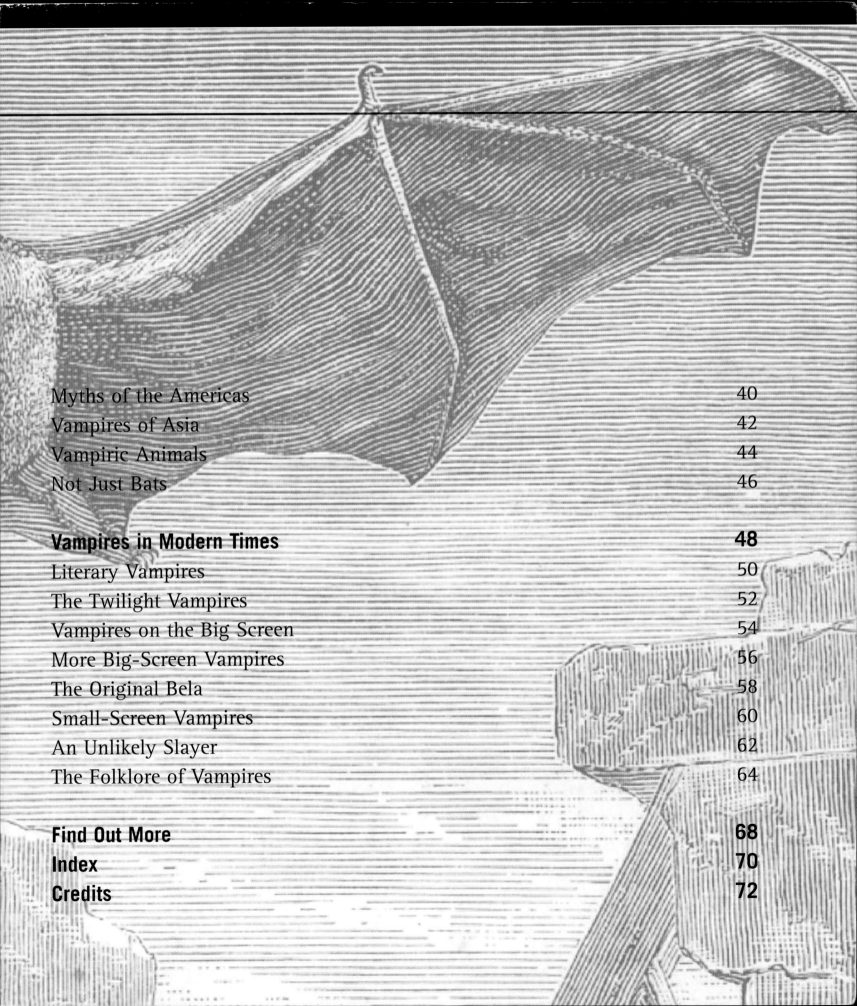

Meet the Vampires

Stories of vampires and vampire-like creatures are as old as recorded history. From the *edimmu* of the ancient Mesopotamians, a fearful creature who could walk through walls to attack its cowering victim, to the ghostly winged *keres* of the ancient Greeks, who haunted blood-soaked battlefields and drank the blood of the wounded, tales of the undead have taken many forms. These stories of ancient blood drinkers can also be found throughout the world and in almost every culture.

Read on and learn about these ancient creatures and the myths and legends surrounding them.

Vampires are not just men. Often, beautiful young women turn into evil, bloodthirsty demons.

Many cultures have undead demons that drink the blood of humans, such as those of Bali and Thailand. Above are colorful masks of vampire-like demons with long, pointy fangs.

Then, travel forward in time and explore the vampire legends of Eastern Europe. These legends gave rise to the vampire that we know today. Journey through the dark, forested mountains of Transylvania and meet the original Count Dracula, a warrior prince whose favorite method of execution was impalement on a dull stake. Explore the gloomy, deserted castle perched high on a mountaintop, where he once lived and ruled, and visit the island monastery rumored to be his final resting place.

Next, read how the myths of Eastern Europe gave rise to the modern vampires. Follow the vampire's dramatic transformation from a hideous, cadaverous creature to an elegant, charismatic figure, attired in evening clothes. Discover the literary sources of Count Dracula and other

modern vampires, and read the story of how the vampire made its way from myth to literary figure and then to the big screen.

Finally, get to know the modern vampire, its habits and its habitats, and its strengths, weaknesses, vulnerabilities, and supernatural powers. Read about modern representations of vampires in best-selling books, hit movies, and popular television series, and find all the sources you need to become a vampire expert.

So, dear reader, continue on if you dare. But beware! Your journey will take you to distant lands and far-off places—to the rain-washed beaches of Forks, Washington, and the sandy dunes of the sun-seared Sahara. And you will discover, to your dismay, that graveyards at the witching hour and secluded villages on stormy nights are not the only places that vampires like to visit!

Watch out for misty cemeteries, such as this one below—especially at night when the undead may decide to leave their graves and hunt for human prey!

Some vampires, such as this one, are ghastly creatures with yellow eyes and clawlike fingernails.

Ancient Blood

The fang-baring, tuxedo-wearing vampires we know today come down to us from the Eastern European tradition. But long before we knew about these ghouls, we had tales of ancient blood-sucking demons who feasted on the blood of the living!

Ancient Mesopotamia, known as the "cradle of civilization," was located in Western Asia, between the Tigris and Euphrates Rivers. This region now makes up parts of Iran, Syria, and Iraq. Mesopotamia included the Sumerian, Babylonian, Akkadian, and Assyrian empires.

The Mesopotamian religions included beliefs in many gods, goddesses, demons, and spirits. Some were evil, blood-drinking beings, such as the Sumerian demon Lilitu, the Babylonian goddess Lamashtu, and the Akkadian *gallu* demons.

Read on and take a journey back in time—if you dare. Visit the great pyramids of Egypt and the crowded forums of Greece and Rome. But beware! They may not have been called "vampires," but these ancient demon blood drinkers were a thirsty bunch!

Demons of Mesopotamia

Known as the "cradle of civilization," Mesopotamia was the rich land between the Tigris and Euphrates Rivers that became the site of the first urban and agricultural communities. During the Bronze Age (3300–1200 BCE), Mesopotamia included the Sumerian, Akkadian, Babylonian, and Assyrian empires. In Mesopotamian mythology, vampire-like demons were not uncommon. Many of them were evil, blood-drinking, undead beings.

Storm Demon

Lilitu, later known as Lilith, was a storm demon. She was considered unclean and could also trigger disease. Lilitu was described as a beautiful woman who would use her beauty to beguile and trap her victims.

To a Sumerian, an *edimmu* (also known as an *ekimmu*) was a frightening creature. If you died a violent death, Sumerians believed that you would come back as an *edimmu* and terrorize the living. *Edimmus* could leave their bodies and walk through walls to attack their victims.

THE ERASER

LAMASHTU means "she who erases."

Bloodthirsty Babylonians

In Babylonian mythology, the goddess Lamashtu was the daughter of the sky god Anu. Lamashtu was a wicked, blood-sucking being, who liked to kidnap babies and drink their fresh, young blood. She could also cause nightmares and make people ill. Unlike Lilitu, she was not beautiful. She had the head of a lion and the body of a donkey!

Kidnapping Vampire

A *gallu* demon was another kind of fearful female demon in Mesopotamian mythology. *Gallu* demons, like Lamashtu, enjoyed kidnapping children and drinking their blood.

OUT, DEMON, OUT

BABYLONIANS USED TRADITIONAL medicine to heal the sick. But if a person could not be cured by traditional means, physicians would turn to exorcism. The idea was to rid the patient of evil curses or spirits thought to be the cause of the illness. The rite of exorcism chased demons or other evil spirits out of a possessed person's body. The person who performed the exorcism, known as an exorcist, was usually considered a holy person. To chase the demon out, the exorcist may have prayed over a possessed person and used special chants, gestures, and materials, such as holy water and charms.

● Mari

GALLU
Akkad
One of the jobs of a *gallu* demon? Drag hapless victims down to the underworld.

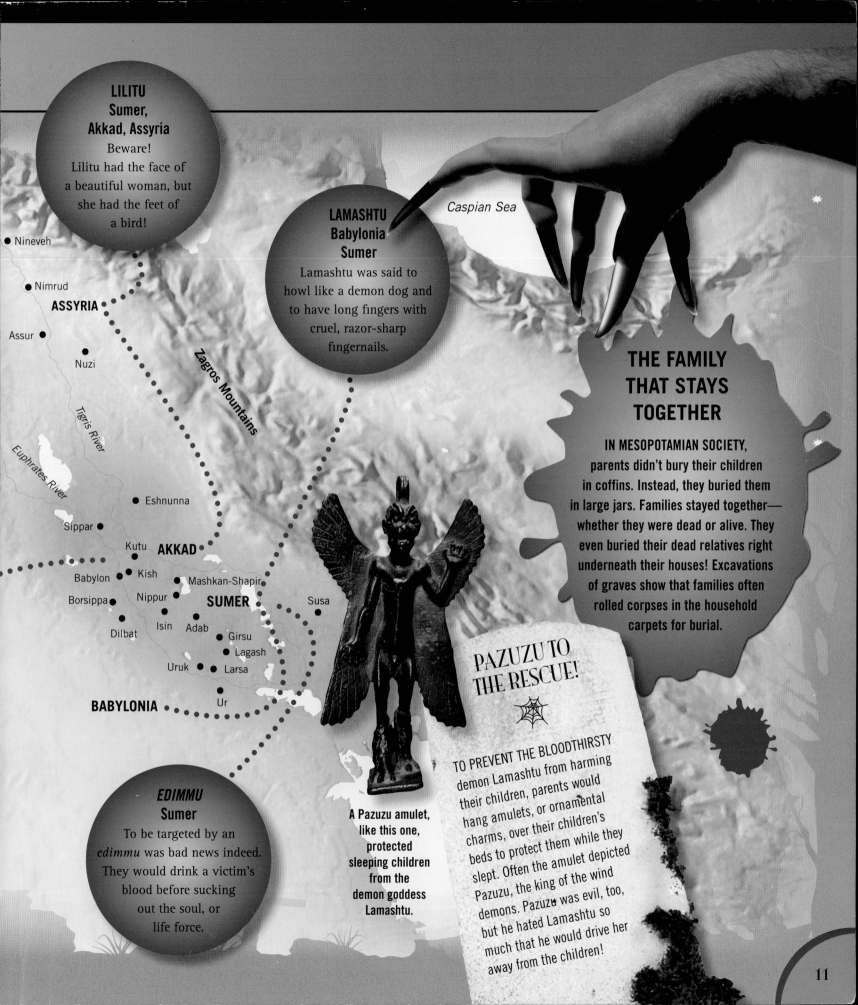

LILITU
Sumer, Akkad, Assyria
Beware! Lilitu had the face of a beautiful woman, but she had the feet of a bird!

- Nineveh
- Nimrud
ASSYRIA
- Assur
- Nuzi

Zagros Mountains

Tigris River

Euphrates River

LAMASHTU
Babylonia
Sumer
Lamashtu was said to howl like a demon dog and to have long fingers with cruel, razor-sharp fingernails.

Caspian Sea

- Eshnunna
- Sippar
- Kutu **AKKAD**
- Babylon • Kish
- Borsippa • Nippur • Mashkan-Shapir
- Dilbat • Isin Adab **SUMER** • Susa
- • Girsu
- • Lagash
- Uruk • • Larsa
BABYLONIA • Ur

THE FAMILY THAT STAYS TOGETHER

IN MESOPOTAMIAN SOCIETY, parents didn't bury their children in coffins. Instead, they buried them in large jars. Families stayed together—whether they were dead or alive. They even buried their dead relatives right underneath their houses! Excavations of graves show that families often rolled corpses in the household carpets for burial.

EDIMMU
Sumer
To be targeted by an *edimmu* was bad news indeed. They would drink a victim's blood before sucking out the soul, or life force.

A Pazuzu amulet, like this one, protected sleeping children from the demon goddess Lamashtu.

PAZUZU TO THE RESCUE!

TO PREVENT THE BLOODTHIRSTY demon Lamashtu from harming their children, parents would hang amulets, or ornamental charms, over their children's beds to protect them while they slept. Often the amulet depicted Pazuzu, the king of the wind demons. Pazuzu was evil, too, but he hated Lamashtu so much that he would drive her away from the children!

Vampires of the Ancient World

The belief in blood as a source of power is as old as humankind itself. But before blood drinkers got the name "vampire," they were simply known as gods, demons, and spirits.

Egyptian Vampires

Sekhmet was a vampire-like goddess in the mythology of ancient Egypt (approximately 2690 BCE to 525 BCE). Her name means "she who is powerful" or "the mighty one." She was also called the "scarlet lady," because of her lust for blood.

Sekhmet had the body of a woman and the head of a lion. She wore clothing of crimson red—the color of fresh blood.

She had more than one aspect, or persona, but one of her most powerful aspects was that of a wrathful killer, who drank the blood of her enemies.

Sekhmet, the lion-head goddess of Egypt, was also known as the Mistress of the Dead and the Lady of Slaughter.

KERES

THE *KERES* (OR *CERES*) were dark, bloodthirsty demons from the mythology of ancient Greece (approximately 1100 BCE to 146 BCE). *Keres* were death spirits who attacked the dying or wounded.

Keres would grab their victims with large claws and talons and then drink their blood. According to legend, once the victim was dead, his soul would travel to Hades. The wicked *keres* often appeared at scenes of carnage or battle—where there was plenty of blood to go around.

SHADES OF EVIL

THE SHADES are vampire-like beings mentioned in the *Odyssey*, an epic about Odysseus, a Greek king and warrior. The legendary Greek writer Homer told this tale of the king's wanderings.

Shades are insubstantial beings, meaning that they have no physical bodies. They must consume blood to take on physical form and communicate with the living.

When Odysseus goes to Hades, the underworld, he sacrifices a lamb so that the shades can drink its blood. After that, the shades are able to talk to him.

DOORWAY OF THE DOOMED

ANCIENT GREEKS THOUGHT that the volcanic crater called Avernus at Lake Avernus in Italy was the entranceway to Hades. Hades was the name of the Greek and Roman underworld, or land of the dead.

Bon appetit! Some vampires enjoy flesh sandwiches.

Dangerous Beauty

In ancient Greek mythology, Empusa was considered an especially frightening demon. She was the daughter of Hecate, the goddess of witchcraft and sorcery.

Empusa had the power to transform herself into a beautiful woman to attack her unsuspecting prey. She would then reveal her true demon form and feast on the blood of her victims.

Roman Mythology

The mythology of ancient Rome (approximately 500 BCE to 476 CE) was similar to Greek mythology in many ways. The Romans, however, had a few demons of their own. One was the *strix*, a name that comes from the Greek word for "owl." This creature was a bird of the night that attacked humans and consumed their flesh— but first it drank its victims' blood.

DID YOU KNOW?

In ancient Greek society, mothers would often use the threat of Lamia to get their children to behave—just like your mom might warn you about the bogeyman.

A MOTHER'S REVENGE

GREEK MYTHOLOGY had other female demons who dined on blood. Lamia was the daughter of Poseidon, the god of the oceans. Lamia had a love affair with Zeus, the king of the gods, and this made Zeus' wife, Hera, angry.

According to legend, Hera took revenge on Lamia by killing her children. Lamia went mad with grief, turning into a vengeful monster. At night she preyed upon human children and drained them of blood while they slept.

Lamia's grief over the death of her children turned her into a crazed monster: half serpent, half woman.

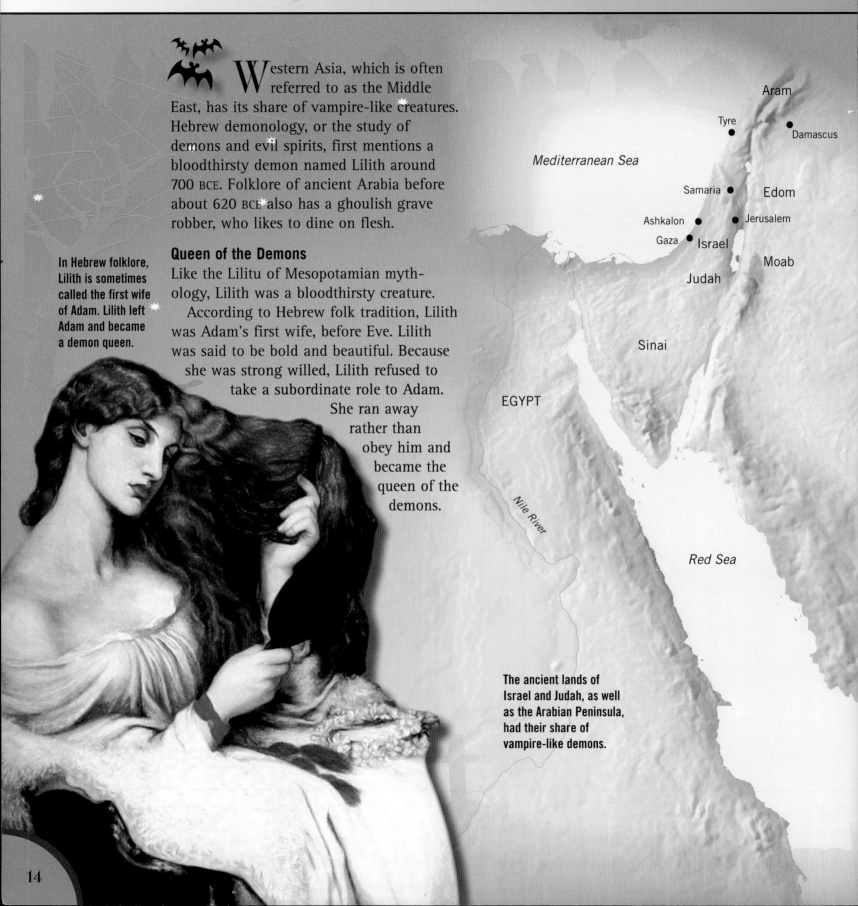

Western Asia, which is often referred to as the Middle East, has its share of vampire-like creatures. Hebrew demonology, or the study of demons and evil spirits, first mentions a bloodthirsty demon named Lilith around 700 BCE. Folklore of ancient Arabia before about 620 BCE also has a ghoulish grave robber, who likes to dine on flesh.

In Hebrew folklore, Lilith is sometimes called the first wife of Adam. Lilith left Adam and became a demon queen.

Queen of the Demons

Like the Lilitu of Mesopotamian myth-ology, Lilith was a bloodthirsty creature.

According to Hebrew folk tradition, Lilith was Adam's first wife, before Eve. Lilith was said to be bold and beautiful. Because she was strong willed, Lilith refused to take a subordinate role to Adam. She ran away rather than obey him and became the queen of the demons.

Aram

Tyre

Damascus

Mediterranean Sea

Samaria

Edom

Ashkalon

Jerusalem

Gaza

Israel

Moab

Judah

Sinai

EGYPT

Nile River

Red Sea

The ancient lands of Israel and Judah, as well as the Arabian Peninsula, had their share of vampire-like demons.

Desert Demons

The *ghul* is an evil *djinn*, or genie, a creature from Arabic folklore. The *ghul* dwelled in the desert and haunted desolate and lonely places. The word *ghul* means "demon" in Arabic.

The *ghul* was a shape-shifter who used this ability to lure the unwary to their deaths. The *ghul* ate the flesh of its victims and particularly enjoyed the tender flesh of young children. When the *ghul* couldn't get its hands on fresh flesh, it robbed graves and ate the decomposing dead!

Arabian Peninsula

The *estrie*, a type of witch, could turn into a hawk so that she could catch prey from above.

WITCHY VAMPIRES

Hebrew demonology also includes the *estrie*. The *estrie* was a witch-vampire who craved the blood of the living—especially that of children. An *estrie* could fly and would swoop down on her unsuspecting victims. She was able to shape-shift, or change her appearance. This ability to slither around as a snake or fly off as a hawk aided her in her pursuit of prey.

GHOULISH TALES

GHULS FIRST APPEAR in the famous collection of Arabian folk tales *One Thousand and One Nights*, in the story "The History of Gherib and His Brother Agib." The European version of this collection also gave us some of our favorite fictional characters, including Aladdin, Ali Baba, and Sinbad the Sailor.

In Arabic folklore, *ghuls* were evil, undead shape-shifters. They haunted graveyards and feasted on corpses. The English word "ghoul" traces its roots back to these demons.

15

Blood of Yore

In ancient times, the name "vampire" did not yet exist. Vampire-like activities, such as returning from the dead and drinking blood, were attributed to demons, spirits, and gods. The name itself comes from the Serbian word *vampir*, but blood-sucking, undead demons went by many names in Eastern Europe, including *strigoi* in Romania, *strzyga* in Poland, and *vrykolakas* in Greece.

The Slavic peoples of Eastern Europe, which include Belarusians, Bulgarians, Czechs, Croats, Macedonians, Moravians, Poles, Russians, Slovaks, Serbs, and Ukrainians, among others, had many vampire legends. And vampires in Slavic folklore were much more complicated than the vampires we know today. They could also be created in many different ways.

Often vampires were thought to be the spirits of evil people or people who had committed suicide or died violent deaths. Most unusual perhaps is that they could be witches or even werewolves who had died and returned as vampires. And a vampire or werewolf bite could turn a human into a vampire. Finally, possession by evil spirits could turn you into the undead.

Slavic Undead

Vampire legends, as most of us know them, come from the Slavic peoples of Eastern Europe. Although these legends were not written down until the early eighteenth century, they are probably based on much older stories.

The causes of vampirism in the Slavic tradition are many and varied. Slavic folklore in the northern areas of Eastern Europe differed from folklore of the southern parts. Slavic vampires, strangely enough, were also said to transform themselves into butterflies rather than bats.

Pretty and harmless? Think again. Slavic vampires morphed into butterflies. Now that's a good disguise!

Northern Vampire Fears

In northern Russia, you could become a vampire by living an immoral life or by not being buried with the proper rituals. You could also become a vampire if a bird flew over your corpse or your empty grave.

Dead and Alive

Romanian vampires came in many different types and had many different names. One type was the *moroi*, which means "nightmare." *Moroi* were usually said to be phantoms that left the grave to steal the energy from the living.

GYPSY LORE

In Roma folklore of the Romany, or Gypsy, people, there were many tales of vampires and vampire hunters. One type of vampire was the *mullo*, which means, "one who is dead." *Mullos* returned from the dead for many reasons and usually targeted family members or people who had wronged them in life. If you died alone, you could come back as a *mullo*. If a corpse had begun to decompose before burial, then that person could also come back as a *mullo*. In Roma tradition, dogs, cats, and even plants could become vampires!

THE UNDEAD

THE DEAD OR UNDEAD *STRIGOI*, called *strigoi mort*, became vampires by rising from the grave and preying upon the living. These *strigoi*, moreover, liked to prey on family members! Unlike the modern vampire, the *strigoi* preferred to bite their victims over the heart or between the eyes.

One way to become a *strigoi viu* was to be born with red hair and blue eyes. This combination apparently puts one at risk for becoming a vampire.

One sip of blood is all it takes to turn into a vampire. In Slavic lore, both *strigoi* and *moroi* left their graves to prey on the living.

BECOMING A VAMPIRE

IN THE EASTERN SLAVIC TRADITION, people could become vampires even before they were dead. While alive, they could engage in vampire activities, like the drinking of blood.

In the southern Slavic tradition, it was believed that you became a vampire through a long, complicated process.

First, the spirit of the dead person would gain strength from sucking the blood of its victims.

Over the next 40 days, the vampire spirit would take on a human form identical to the one it had while alive.

Finally, the vampire would rise from its grave and begin a new life.

These vampires, if male, could have children with human women. The children would not be vampires, but instead *dhampirs*, or vampire hunters. *Dhampirs* had special abilities to recognize and kill vampires.

A second type was the *strigoi*, which could be either a living or dead creature. *Strigoi viu* were alive and had never died. They could leave their bodies and band together with other *strigoi viu* to prey on normal people. They enjoyed the blood of animals as well as humans.

You could become a *strigoi viu* in many ways. One way was to be born the seventh child in a family. If the seventh child was a boy, and all six of his siblings were girls, he would become a *strigoi*. The same would happen to a girl born seventh who had only older brothers.

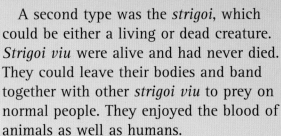

DID YOU KNOW?

In Bram Stoker's novel *Dracula*, Count Dracula named his pet wolves Strigoi and Moroi.

Tales From Eastern Europe

Slavic traditions of vampires extended throughout Eastern Europe, from the chilly forests of Poland to the warmer shores of Greece.

Double Trouble

Polish folklore had tales of the *strzyga*. This vampire had been born human—but had two sets of teeth, two hearts, and two souls. At death, one of the souls passed on to the afterlife, but the other hung around earth. It would leave its grave to prey on the living.

One of the versions of the legend says that *strzyga* were undead babies. A stillborn child would return from the grave to live in the forest. There, bands of *strzyga* attacked anyone unlucky enough to pass through the woods after dark. *strzyga* loved to feast on their victims' insides! The best way to kill a *strzyga* was to behead it. Preferably, in one stroke.

FALSE PROTECTION

FROM THE MIDDLE AGES up to the eighteenth century, charlatans, or con artists, traveled around Eastern Europe posing as *dhampirs*. Villages would pay them to rid the surrounding area of vampires. Not a bad way to make a living, considering vampires didn't really exist.

Greek Vrykolakas

The *vrykolakas* is a vampire from Greek folklore. You could become a *vrykolakas* by dying after being expelled from the Eastern Orthodox Church or by being buried in unconsecrated ground. If a cat jumped over your grave, or if you ate meat from a sheep killed by a wolf, you too were at risk.

Greek folklore also included many tales of werewolves, or lycanthropes. Many people believed that werewolves could come back as vampires after death.

My, what big teeth you have! The Greeks had tales of werewolves that were humans who turned into wolves during full moons. To make matters worse, these creatures might not even find peace after death. Some of them returned as blood-sucking vampires!

Warsaw

Polish-Lithuanian Commonwealth

STRZYGA

Tsardom of Russia

STRIGOI

Austria

Moldavia

MOROI

Khanate of the Crimea

Budapest

Transylvania

Bucharest

Carpathian Mountains

Sighisoara

Wallachia

MULLO

Tirgoviste

Black Sea

Danube River

DHAMPIR

Constantinople

Ottoman Empire

The belief in vampires and other undead beings was once widespread throughout Eastern Europe.

VRYKOLAKAS

Aegean Sea

Adriatic Sea

Athens

Greece

Door-Knockers

The *vrykolakas* were also known as "door-knockers." *Vrykolakas* liked to roam the countryside, playing tricks on villagers—and worse.

They would knock on cottage doors and call out the resident's name. If no one answered, they would move on to the next house. Anyone expecting company had better beware. Answering the first knock or call meant that the person would soon die—and return as a *vrykolakas.*

WARDING OFF *VRYKOLAKAS*

Christian crosses and bread blessed by a priest were believed to provide protection from vampires. One sure way to kill a *vrykolakas* was to trap it in its grave and cut off its head. Another surefire way: pin the vampire to its coffin by driving iron nails though its heart!

The Real-Life Dracula

Fans of the fictional Dracula will probably recognize the real-life Dracula, otherwise known as "Vlad Dracula" and "Vlad Tepes."

Vlad Dracula is a historical figure who is said to have inspired the character of the evil Count Dracula in the famous Bram Stoker novel *Dracula*.

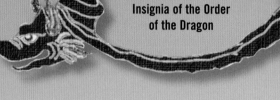

Insignia of the Order of the Dragon

Son of the Dragon

Vlad Dracula was born in what is present-day Romania in the year 1431. His father was known as Vlad Dracul. *Dracul*, in Romanian means "dragon," although it is also sometimes translated as "devil."

Vlad Dracula, the real-life inspiration for fictional vampires

HEY, GOOD LOOKING

VLAD DRACULA was described as having green eyes and curly black hair. His portrait hangs in the Gallery of Horrors at Ambras Castle, in Austria. There he stares out at all who pass. Although no one considered Vlad particularly good looking, his brother was known as Radu the Handsome.

GRUESOME WAYS TO DIE

THE NAME *TEPES* is pronounced "tse-pesh" and means "impaler" in the Romanian language. Vlad Dracula became known as Vlad the Impaler because his favorite method of execution was impalement. Impalement is one of the most gruesome ways to die. When a person is impaled, a stake is slowly forced into the body. The stake is first well oiled and shaved, however, so that it will not be too sharp. Victims are meant to suffer and to die a slow, agonizing death.

Under Vlad's instructions the stake was often inserted between the legs to eventually emerge through the victim's mouth. For variety, some victims were impaled upside down. Vlad would often have his victims arranged on stakes in geometric patterns. He liked to have the highest-ranking victims impaled on the tallest stakes.

Vlad didn't just impale: he employed many other horrible forms of punishment and execution. He is accused of having his victims skinned alive, boiled alive, slow roasted alive, buried alive, and thrown to wild animals to be ripped to shreds. Executions included hanging, strangling, decapitation, and burning at the stake. Punishments included blinding with hot irons, scalping, and the cutting off of noses, ears, and limbs.

The city of Tirgoviste was Vlad's childhood home and scene of some of his more horrible acts as a ruling prince.

DID YOU KNOW?

Despite his evil reputation, in 2006, Vlad was voted one of "100 Greatest Romanians" in the *Mari Români* television series.

Vlad's father was given the name Dracul when he was inducted into the Order of the Dragon. This order was a secret group of knights who pledged to fight against the Turks. The name Dracula means "son of Dracul" or "son of the dragon." Dracula was Vlad's last name.

Held Hostage

During the Middle Ages, Romania was divided into three areas that were ruled by three princes: Wallachia, Moldavia, and Transylvania. Vlad's father was a prince of Wallachia. Vlad spent part of his youth at his father's palace at Tirgoviste, Wallachia. He did not get to grow up there, though.

While still young, Vlad spent time as a hostage to the Turkish sultan Murad II. After political enemies in Wallachia assassinated Vlad's father and brother, the sultan released Vlad. In 1456, after a long, hard fight, Vlad seized the throne of Wallachia.

Vlad the Impaler

Many different stories are told about Vlad Dracula and the cruel deeds he is accused of perpetrating during his six-year reign.

For example, to avenge the death of his father and brother, who had been buried alive, Vlad invited his noblemen, called boyars, and their families to a feast on Easter Sunday 1459. He arrested them all and impaled the old and infirm on wooden stakes. He forced the remaining boyars to hike more than 50 miles to the town of Poenari. The ones who survived the grueling journey were put to work building a castle.

The fortress they built overlooks the Arges River and is called Poenari Castle. It is also sometimes called Castle Dracula. Parts of the castle still stand today.

The Long Walk

To reach Poenari Castle, you must climb 1,500 steps. At the top, you can look down on the Arges River. The Arges is sometimes called "the Lady's River." It got this nickname because Vlad's wife is said to have leaped to her death from the castle in order to avoid capture by the invading Turks. Filmmaker Francis Ford Coppola re-created this scene in the movie *Bram Stoker's Dracula*.

THE COUNT

In the novel *Dracula*, Dracula is called Count Dracula. In real life, Vlad Dracula had the title of *voivode* or *waywode*, meaning "war leader," "war lord," or "warrior prince." This Slavic title meant that Vlad Dracula was the chief commander of the military in Wallachia. The English translation is sometimes "prince," "duke," or even "count." Therefore, the real Dracula could actually be called Count Dracula.

FEAST OF DEATH

VLAD CONSIDERED THE POOR and beggars useless. According to one story, he invited the poor and sick people of Wallachia to come to his court for a feast. When they arrived, he first fed them and then ordered the great feasting hall boarded up and set on fire.

The ruins of Vlad's Poenari Castle sit high on a mountain.

A Fitting Death

Vlad Dracula died in a battle with the Turks in 1476. Some historians say that disloyal Wallachian boyars assassinated Vlad during the fighting. His head was chopped off and presented to the sultan in Constantinople as proof that he was dead.

His body was buried near the Romanian city of Bucharest, at Snagov Monastery. His tomb was opened in 1931, but it was empty. Perhaps Vlad Dracula was more than just the inspiration for the famous vampire. Perhaps he was the real thing!

UNTHINKABLE NUMBERS

A PERSON COULD BE IMPALED in Vlad Dracula's Wallachia for almost any crime. Stealing, or even lying, could be grounds for impalement. Some legends claim that Vlad Dracula impaled between 40,000 and 100,000 people.

FOREST OF THE IMPALED

VLAD IS SAID to have executed thousands of Turkish prisoners at one time by impaling them on stakes that lined the road to his capital city of Tirgoviste. The sight of the rotting bodies was too much for the usually fearless Sultan Mohammed II, the conqueror of Constantinople. Mohammed had planned to invade Wallachia and make it part of the Turkish empire, but the impaled corpses were so horrifying that he quickly turned around and headed back home. This horrible act became known as the "Forest of the Impaled" and is captured on woodblock carvings made in Vlad's day.

A bust of Vlad stands in a courtyard near his birthplace. Vlad Dracula is considered by many Romanians to be a national hero. He is credited with defending his people from invaders and championing the common people against the rich and powerful.

CRUELTY UNMATCHED

NO ONE WAS SPARED VLAD'S grisly tortures. Men, women, and even innocent young children were impaled and left to suffer until they died. Infants often merited special treatment—they were impaled on stakes that were forced through their mothers' chests.

The Haunts of Vlad Dracula

Many of Vlad Dracula's haunts have survived into the twenty-first century, even if some of them, such as Poenari Castle, are little more than ruins. Here are some of the landmark locations in the life of this cruel and mysterious prince.

In această casă a locuit intre anii 1431–1435, domnitorul Țării Românești **VLAD DRACUL**, fiul lui Mircea cel Bătrin.

CARPATHIAN MOUNTAINS

In 1462, Vlad fled Poenari Castle through a secret passageway and hid in the Carpathian Mountains to avoid capture by the Turks.

SIGHISOARA

Place of Vlad's birth and one of the best-preserved medieval towns in Europe. The house where Vlad was born still stands with a plaque calling attention to the infamous infant.

DRACULA'S CASTLE

Bran Castle sits on the border between Transylvania and Wallachia. Although it's known as "Dracula's Castle," Vlad never lived in it—it's called that because Bram Stoker made it the home of his fictional Dracula.

Transylvania

Oriental Carpathians

Moldava River

Roman

Baccau

Dimbraveni

Sighisoara

Brasov

Meridional Carpathians

Tirgu Jiu

Tirgoviste

Ploiesti

Turnu Severin

Slatina

Bucharest

Danube River

Wallachia

DID YOU KNOW?

The Carpathian Mountains is the largest mountain range in Europe. The Carpathians are also the largest habitat for the European wolf. And more wolves can be found in Romania than anywhere else. This may be why, perhaps, Romanian folklore has as many tales of werewolves as it does of vampires.

VLAD'S "PALACE"

Built to serve as a watchtower by Vlad, Chindia Tower lies within the complex known as the Royal Court of Tirgoviste.

Chisinau

Moldavia

Dnesti River

POENARI CASTLE

The castle built by his imprisoned Romanian nobles, who were called "boyars."

Sulina

SNAGOV MONASTERY

The monastery is built on a small island, and you can only get there by boat. According to legend, Dracula's headless body was buried in a tomb in front of the altar.

Constanta

27

Vampire Hunters

During the eighteenth century, many people believed in vampires, especially in parts of Eastern Europe. Folks were so afraid of vampires that they actually unearthed graves and mutilated corpses, beheading, burning them, or driving stakes through the hearts. Innocent people were accused of being vampires. Government officials and members of the church often stepped in to investigate claims of vampirism. And although prominent figures spoke out against the existence of vampires, people still believed.

The Hunt Ends

In 1755, Empress Maria Theresa of Austria ordered her personal physician, Gerard van Swieten, to make a determination on whether vampires existed. When van Swieten concluded that vampires did not exist, the empress prohibited the digging up and mutilation of dead bodies. The prohibition had the desired effect, and, by the late 1700s, the hunt for vampires finally came to an end.

BETTER SAFE THAN SORRY

VAMPIRE KILLING KITS were extremely popular in Europe during the 1800s. These kits provided all the tools necessary to kill a vampire: stake, cross, garlic powder, gun, and holy water. Everything was packed in a portable case so that it could be conveniently carried. Apparently, you never knew when you would run into a vampire. It should come as no surprise that these kits are collector's items today.

Who wouldn't want one!

I NOW PRONOUNCE YOU . . . VAMPIRE

AN INTERESTING CASE INVOLVED a man named Arnold Paole. Paole was a Serbian soldier who was accused of returning from the dead as a vampire and attacking his neighbors. It was claimed that he had killed 16 villagers. Austrian authorities investigating the case "officially" confirmed that vampires did, in fact, exist. These findings were published in 1732 and widely spread throughout Europe.

Travelers journeying from Boston to Transylvania in 1840 were well prepared to face anything that came their way, including vampires!

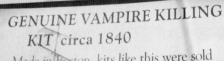

GENUINE VAMPIRE KILLING KIT circa 1840
Made in Boston, kits like this were sold to people sailing to Transylvania - the legendary home of vampires.
BELIEVE IT OR NOT!

NEIGHBORLY RELATIONS

There are many stories of vampire accusations against innocent people. One well-documented story is that of Peter Plogojowitz, a Serbian peasant. In 1725, a local official from the village of Kisilova filed a report, claiming that Plogojowitz had died and come back as a vampire. Frombald, the official, accused the vampire Plogojowitz of murdering his own son, as well as nine of his fellow villagers. Even Plogojowitz's wife claimed that her dead husband had returned from the grave and was visiting her at night. Fearful villagers, with Frombald and a local priest present, dug up Plogojowitz's body and drove a stake through his heart. Frombald noted in his report that as the stake plunged into the heart fresh blood spurted out of the corpse's mouth and ears. So, for good measure, the villagers burned the corpse. The story was even reported in Austrian newspapers.

Not all *dhampirs* know advanced martial arts. Blade does, and he uses it to kill evil vampires and other demons of the night.

Little Vampires

Male vampires, in the Roma tradition, could have children with human women. These children, as in the Slavic tradition, would be *dhampirs*, or vampire hunters. If you needed to kill a vampire, you could hire a *dhampir* to do the job. The word *dhampir* means "little vampire."

NOT-SO-LITTLE VAMPS

THE CHARACTER BLADE in the movie *Blade* is a type of *dhampir*. His mother was a human who had been bitten by a vampire moments before Blade was born. Because he is a *dhampir*, Blade has all the strengths of a vampire, without the weaknesses. He is able to move about during the day and is nicknamed "day-walker."

The character Connor in the television series *Angel* is also a type of *dhampir*. Like Blade, Connor has the strength of his vampire parents, but he can move about during the day.

Bram Stoker and *Dracula*

Bram Stoker created the famous vampire Count Dracula.

Bram Stoker is best known as the author of the horror classic *Dracula*. Stoker, whose full first name was Abraham, was born on November 8, 1847, in Ireland, the third of seven children. Stoker was ill as a child and spent most of his time in bed until he was 7. Some people think that his many years abed, reading stories and Irish fairy tales, led to his love of horror and fantasy fiction.

In 1878, Stoker married and moved to London. There he took a job as the manager of the Lyceum Theatre. To supplement his income, he wrote novels, the most famous of which is *Dracula*. *Dracula* was first published in 1897. Stoker spent many years researching European folklore and tales of vampires before writing *Dracula*.

VAMPIRE VACATIONS

TODAY YOU CAN GO ON DRACULA TOURS in Romania. These sightseeing tours include trips to the gloomy remains of Vlad the Impaler's mountaintop fortress at Poenari. There are also stops at gypsy bazaars where you can buy Dracula doll souvenirs. Tours include trips to the forested Carpathians and a reenactment of the journey Jonathan Harker took in the novel. You can also visit the Golden Crown Inn, mentioned in the book, and even order the same meal as Harker: "Robber Steak," made of beef with bits of onion and bacon, seasoned with red pepper.

DRACULA, THE NOVEL

BRAM STOKER'S NOVEL is set in Transylvania and told through a series of diaries and letters. Jonathan Harker is an English solicitor, or lawyer, who travels to Transylvania to conduct a real estate transaction for the mysterious Count Dracula. Dracula travels to England where he is unmasked as a vampire by Dr. Abraham van Helsing. Dracula flees back to Transylvania where he is staked and destroyed.

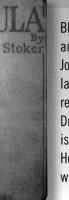

Jonathan Harker's journey took him from London, England, and across Europe by train to Bistritz, Romania. From there, he took a horse-drawn coach through the rugged Borgo Pass to Count Dracula's eerie castle.

Frank Langella playing Dracula on Broadway in 1977. When *Dracula* was first performed on the stage, the actor playing the count had to provide his own costume for the role: evening clothes. He later complained that the cost was way too high!

WHY WASTE A GOOD CHAPTER?

"DRACULA'S GUEST," A short story published after Stoker's death, was really a chapter from *Dracula* that had been deleted to shorten the novel. It tells the story of Harker's journey to Castle Dracula on Walpurgis Night and his encounter with a female vampire. This story would later serve as the basis for the 1936 movie *Dracula's Daughter*.

Look out, she'll get you! Although Stoker cut "Dracula's Guest" from the original novel, the chapter inspired *Dracula's Daughter*, a sequel to the *1931* hit movie *Dracula*.

WALPURGIS NIGHT

WALPURGIS NIGHT, celebrated April 30 to May 1, mentioned in "Dracula's Guest," is believed to be the one night of the year when the barrier between the living and the dead grows thin. This allows the dead to cross over and walk among us. Some say that on this night witches meet with their master, the Devil, to celebrate evil in all its forms.

Dracula's Inspirations

She may have looked innocent, but Elizabeth Báthory, shown at right, had a taste for blood.

Bram Stoker took pieces of the folklore from many countries, including Romania and even the United States, and mixed them in his rich imagination to come up with the most famous vampire of all.

The Blood Countess

Stories of the Blood Countess, Elizabeth Báthory, who lived from 1560 to 1614 in Hungary, may have inspired Bram Stoker. Her uncle and grandfather had both been princes in Transylvania.

According to legend, the countess was a beautiful woman who turned to black magic and witchcraft to preserve her beauty. The countess is accused of torturing and killing more than 600 girls and young women so that she could bathe in their blood. Her tortures were said to include burning or mutilation of hands and faces, freezing, starving, and beatings. She is also said to have employed long, sharp needles in her tortures. The countess was finally arrested and bricked up in a four-room suite, where she lived for four years before dying.

FAIRY TALES

BRAM STOKER may have been influenced by stories of blood-drinking women in Irish folklore when he fashioned his portrait of Dracula's wives in the novel. As a child, Stoker probably heard or read stories about the *sídhe*, fairy women who were bloodsuckers.

The ruins of the once-magnificent Whitby Abbey in Yorkshire, England, inspired Stoker. In the novel, he even has the count use the abbey's graveyard as his sleeping spot. Dracula takes up residence in an unhallowed grave of a suicide victim.

A SECRET SOCIETY

Bram Stoker was said to be a member of a secret occult order society called the Hermetic Order of the Golden Dawn. The order believed in and practiced ritual magic, also known as sorcery. The sinister Aleister Crowley, who wrote books on magic and the occult, was a member, as was the poet William Butler Yeats.

WHAT'S IN A NAME?

STOKER ORIGINALLY CALLED his book about the vampire count "The Un-Dead." He later changed it to "Undead" and finally published the book under the title *Dracula*. The vampire in the novel was first called Count Vampyre. Fortunately, his name was later changed to Count Dracula.

Not all vampires are scary. These friendly-looking vamp souvenirs are found in tourist markets in Transylvania.

THE RHODE ISLAND VAMPIRE

MASSACHUSETTS

RHODE ISLAND

Providence

CONNECTICUT

Exeter, Rhode Island

ATLANTIC OCEAN

STORIES OF VAMPIRES committing foul deeds from the grave can also be found in the United States. During the eighteenth and nineteenth centuries, many people believed in vampires—especially in New England.

One well-documented case occurred in Exeter, Rhode Island, in 1892, and involved a 19-year-old girl named Mercy Brown. Poor Mercy Brown had died from tuberculosis, and her father believed that she had come back to life as a vampire. Her father was sure that vampire Mercy had made her brother Edwin sick. So, one cold winter day, he and the family physician dug up Mercy and cut out her heart. They then burned it and mixed the ashes with water. Then, they gave this "elixir" to the sick child Edwin to drink, hoping that this mixture would cure Edwin of his tuberculosis. Not surprisingly, the cure failed, and Edwin died two months later. This bizarre incident was so well known that Stoker, who lived in England, heard of it and used a version of it in *Dracula*.

DID YOU KNOW?

When Bram Stoker's son, Irving Noel, died, his ashes were placed in the same urn as that of his father.

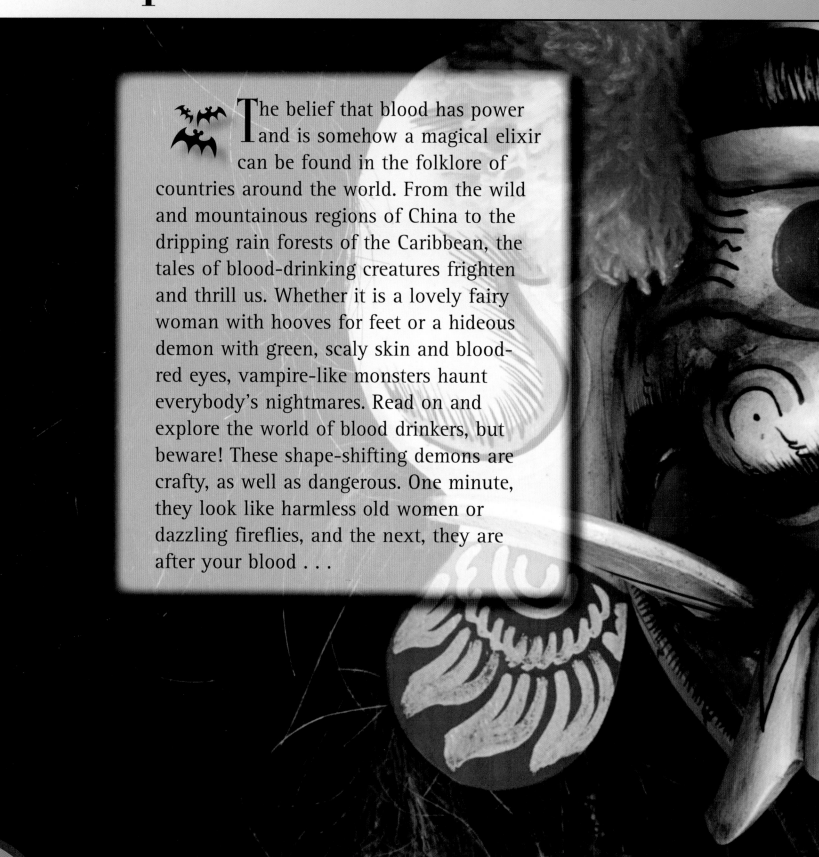

Vampires Around the World

The belief that blood has power and is somehow a magical elixir can be found in the folklore of countries around the world. From the wild and mountainous regions of China to the dripping rain forests of the Caribbean, the tales of blood-drinking creatures frighten and thrill us. Whether it is a lovely fairy woman with hooves for feet or a hideous demon with green, scaly skin and blood-red eyes, vampire-like monsters haunt everybody's nightmares. Read on and explore the world of blood drinkers, but beware! These shape-shifting demons are crafty, as well as dangerous. One minute, they look like harmless old women or dazzling fireflies, and the next, they are after your blood . . .

Celtic Fairy Vampires

The Celts were ancient peoples who once lived in many parts of Europe during the Iron Age (1200 BCE–550 CE). Still, they may be best known as early inhabitants of the British Isles. It's no surprise then that folktales from Ireland and Scotland have many elements in common. One is the belief in beautiful fairy women who are deadly to humans.

Psychic Vampires

Called the *leanan sídhe* in Irish and Manx folklore and *liannan shith* in Scottish folklore, these are beautiful women who prey on human men. *Leanan sídhe* means "fairy sweetheart" in Gaelic, the traditional language of Ireland.

Because of the fairies' beauty, men fall in love with them—and once in love, the poor men slowly go mad and die.

Although they aren't typical vampires, the fairy woman can be considered psychic vampires. The fairies drain the life forces of the men, leaving them empty shells. Rather than drink the blood, a *leanan sídhe* collects it in a great cauldron.

Dancing Vampires

Scottish folklore includes a second deadly vampire-type creature. The *baobhan sith* is also a beautiful woman who preys on humans. Unlike

Scottish Highlands

SCOTLAND

North Sea

NORTHERN IRELAND

Isle of Man

Irish Sea

IRELAND

ENGLAND

WALES

Celtic Sea

Cornwall

English Channel

Brittany

FRANCE

Although many Manx cats have no tails at all, some have stubs like the one shown here.

MAN, WHAT A CAT!

THE ISLE OF MAN is located in the Irish Sea, at the geographical center of the British Isles. The word *Manx* is used to describe the people, customs, or anything else to do with the island. A well-known breed of cat comes from the Isle of Man: the tailless Manx cat.

Although the Celts were once widespread across the continent of Europe, as well as the British Isles (shown above), today "Celtic Europe" usually means the lands surrounding the Irish Sea, as well as Cornwall in England and Brittany, France, on either side of the English Channel.

psychic vampires, the *baobhan sith* drinks the blood of her victims.

Baobhan sith usually appear in groups and like to haunt forests. After dark, they look for young men, who find their beauty irresistible. They are sometimes said to have deer hooves for feet, which they keep hidden under long, flowing gowns. They invite the young men to dance, exhausting them until they collapse. That's when they drain their victims of blood.

The *baobhan sith* have weaknesses that are similar to Eastern European vampires. They cannot stand sunlight. They are creatures of the night and sleep in their coffins in between their meals of blood. Unlike other vampires, these vampires do not use fangs to kill and sip blood. Instead, they use long, clawlike fingernails.

The *baobhan sith* is also known as the White Woman of the Scottish Highlands. So, if you ever visit Scotland, beware of the woods at night and run from beautiful women who look especially pale.

NIGHT OF THE HUNGRY DEAD

IN IRELAND, the Celts once celebrated the *Failte na Marbh* (Festival of the Dead) on October 31. On this night, the dead left their graves to visit their living relatives. These creatures, known as *Marbh Bheo*, or the Night-walking Dead, expected their kin to give them food and drink. If they didn't like what they were offered, they would feed from the veins of the living.

She may be beautiful to look at, but a *leanan sídhe* is a dangerous creature. Sometimes, a *leanan sídhe* will lure a man to her home, which is often in a tower. After she tires of him, she will change him into an animal or a plant.

Leanan sídhe are said to collect their victims' blood in large cauldrons, such as the one shown here. Cauldrons are large cooking pots used to cook over an open fire. We know them best as the pots witches use to brew their potions.

37

The *adze*, a blood-drinking creature of West Africa, can take the form of a firefly, such as the one below.

Africa, home to the Nile, the world's longest river, and the Sahara, the world's largest desert, is also home to frightening tales of demons, devils, and vampire-like creatures. Some of these vampire traditions crossed the Atlantic with African slaves. These traditions mixed with the beliefs of other cultures that settled the islands of the Caribbean Sea to create such fearsome creatures as the *loogaroo* and the *soucouyant*. These creatures may be different from the vampires of Europe, but they are just as dangerous and deadly!

SOUCOUYANT
Trinidad

UNITED STATES

Louisiana

HAITI

CARIBBEAN SEA

GRENADA

LOOGAROO
Haiti, Grenada, United States

TRINIDAD AND TOBAGO

Vampire Fireflies

West Africa has tales of a vampire-like being called the *adze*. This vampire comes from the folklore of the Ewe people of Ghana and Togo. Young people beware! This vampire likes to hunt children and drink their hot, red blood. When hunting its prey, the *adze* changes shape. It appears as a harmless firefly, but it is deadly in its human form.

Forest Vampires

Another vampire-like creature is the *sasabonsam*, or *asasabonsam*. This vampire comes from the Ashanti tradition of the people of southern Ghana, Cote d'Ivoire, and Togo. The *sasabonsam* is said to have teeth of iron and likes to hide in trees, deep in the forest. Should an unwary walker come along, the *sasabonsam* drops down, snatching its victim from above. It has hooked feet and uses them to snare its prey.

The Devil's Payment

The *loogaroo* is a demon common in the folklore of Haiti, Grenada, and other islands in the Caribbean, and in the state of Louisiana in the United States. This creature is a woman who has made a pact with the Devil in exchange for magical abilities. The Devil demands his payments in blood each night, so she must go in search of victims. The *loogaroo* can even leave her body if she needs to and travels about as a glowing fireball. But, it is only when she's collected enough blood from her victims that she can regain her human form.

TWO LOOKS, ONE VAMP

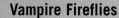

ACCORDING TO ONE LEGEND, THE *sasabonsam* is a hairy creature with big, bloodshot eyes, long legs, and feet pointing both ways. This version of the *sasabonsam* likes to sit on the high branches of a tree and dangle its legs in order to entangle an unwary hunter walking in the forest. In another version of the legend, the *sasabonsam* has the face of a bearded man with horns atop his head. Its body is small and skinny, and its legs are short and twisted. Batlike wings hang beneath its stubby arms, which makes some people wonder if this legend started with some type of gigantic forest bat!

SASABONSAM
Ghana, Togo,
Cote d'Ivoire

ATLANTIC
OCEAN

A F R I C A

COTE
D'IVOIRE

TOGO

GHANA

ADZE
Ghana, Togo

Jump Out of Your Skin

The *soucouyant*, also called a *soucriant*, is a vampire that comes from the folklore of the island of Trinidad. The *soucouyant* lives as an old woman during the day and as a blood-sucking creature at night. She practices black magic. To travel freely at night, the *soucouyant* slips out of her skin and puts it into a bowl called a mortar. Without her skin,

she flies about as a shimmering ball of energy. In this form, she can enter houses by puffing in through the keyholes or other small openings. If she takes too much of her victim's blood, the victim will die and return as a *soucouyant*.

A *soucouyant* must return to her house before the rooster crows at dawn, or she can't get in. To destroy her, you must put salt in the mortar containing her skin. The salt shrinks the skin, keeping the *soucouyant* from slithering back into it—and without her skin she will die.

A *soucouyant* has the ability to abandon her human form and dissolve into a ball of fire. This lets her travel without any boundaries.

A mortar is a strong bowl that is used with a clublike utensil called a pestle to pound substances together. If you found a *soucouyant*'s mortar with her skin in it, you could grind salt into the skin, ruining her chances of fitting back into it!

DID YOU KNOW?

The term *soucouyant* is derived from a French word meaning "to suck."

DON'T LOSE COUNT!

DOORS AND SHUTTERS are no barriers to the *loogaroo*, who can slip through the tiniest chink or smallest space when in her fireball form. To keep her out, scatter rice and sand around your house. The *loogaroo* must stay until she's counted every single grain. Morning will probably come before the counting is over.

Myths of the Americas

From the Maya peoples who once lived in what is now Mexico in North America and Guatemala, Belize, El Salvador, and Honduras in Central America to the Mapuche and Chilota peoples who live in southern Chile in South America, the western hemisphere has its share of tales featuring creepy creatures of the night.

The Maya peoples lived in the range of vampire bats, so it is not surprising that they had a god that was half bat and half human.

Ancient Batman

The Maya civilization lasted about 3,500 years, from 2000 BCE to 1500 CE. The Maya pantheon of gods includes the bat god

WHICH BAT WAS IT?

Most archaeologists believe that Camazotz was based on the common vampire bat (*Desmodus rotundus*), which feeds on the blood of other animals. In 1988, archaeologists even dug up a fossil bat relative of *Desmodus rotundus*—only this one was 25 percent larger than its modern cousin. Still, some think that the false vampire bat (*Vampyrum spectrum*) is the likelier origin of the myth, because it is larger than the common vampire bat and attacks its prey around the head or neck.

Camazotz, whose name can be translated as "death bat" or "snatch bat." Camazotz has the body of a human but the head and wings of a bat. It's possible that giant blood-sucking bats that lived long ago may have given rise to the belief in this particular god. In fact, there is modern fossil evidence that actual giant bats lived and fed in Mexico!

Peg-Leg Vampire

Tunda, or *La Tunda*, is a vampire from the folklore of the people of the Colombian Pacific. Tunda often appears disguised as a family member of her victim. She especially likes to appear as the mother of lost children. She lures her victims deep into the forest, where they meet their deadly fate. Thankfully, her changeling abilities are imperfect. You can spot her because she will always have one wooden leg. So, beware of limping ladies in long skirts!

Hissing Bloodsuckers

The *peuchen* is a vampire from the folk tales of southern Chile. Stories of this creature can be found in the folklore of the Mapuche and Chilota people. This frightening shape-shifter can morph into animal form in an instant. Its favorite shape is that of a flying, hissing snake. Its power is such that its gaze can instantly paralyze prey. Once the prey is immobilized, the *peuchen* swoops in for the blood-sucking frenzy. *Peuchen* are difficult to kill, and you need the assistance of a *machi*, or medicine woman. Only she knows how to put an end to this deadly creature.

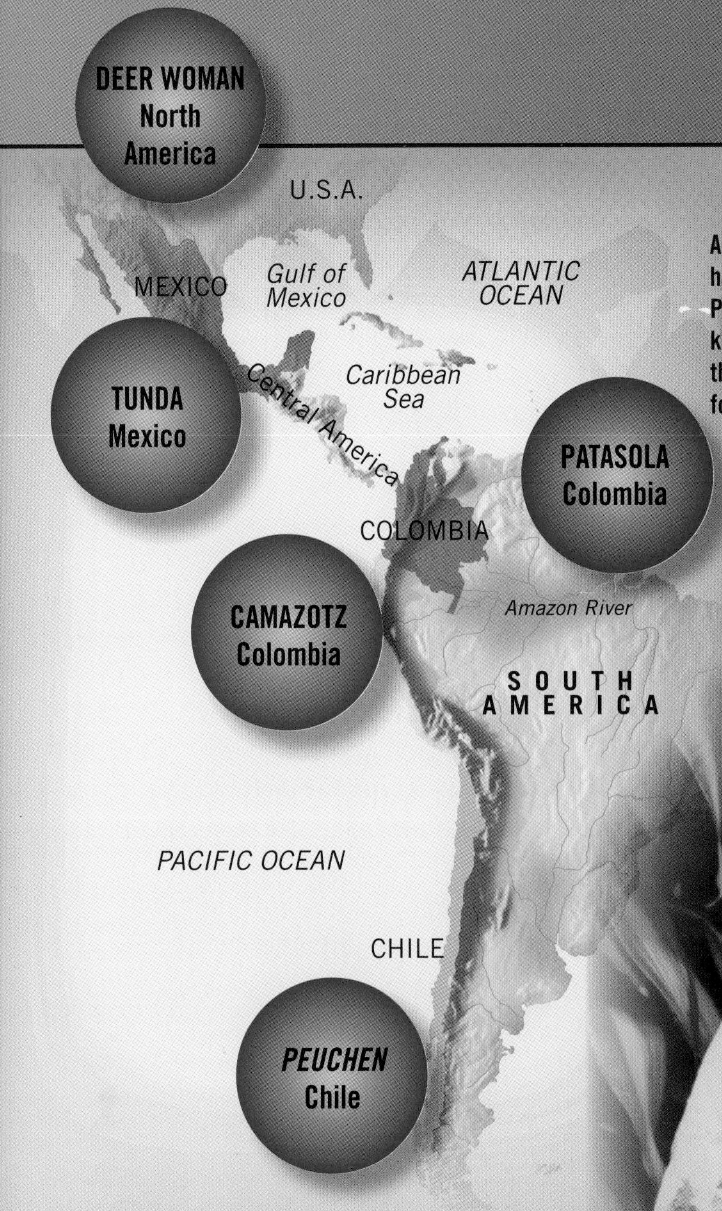

DEER WOMAN
North America

U.S.A.

MEXICO

Gulf of Mexico

ATLANTIC OCEAN

Caribbean Sea

Central America

TUNDA
Mexico

PATASOLA
Colombia

COLOMBIA

CAMAZOTZ
Colombia

Amazon River

SOUTH AMERICA

PACIFIC OCEAN

CHILE

PEUCHEN
Chile

Although she can only hop on her one leg, the hideous hag Patasola is a bloodthirsty killer, looking for victims that pass through her forest home.

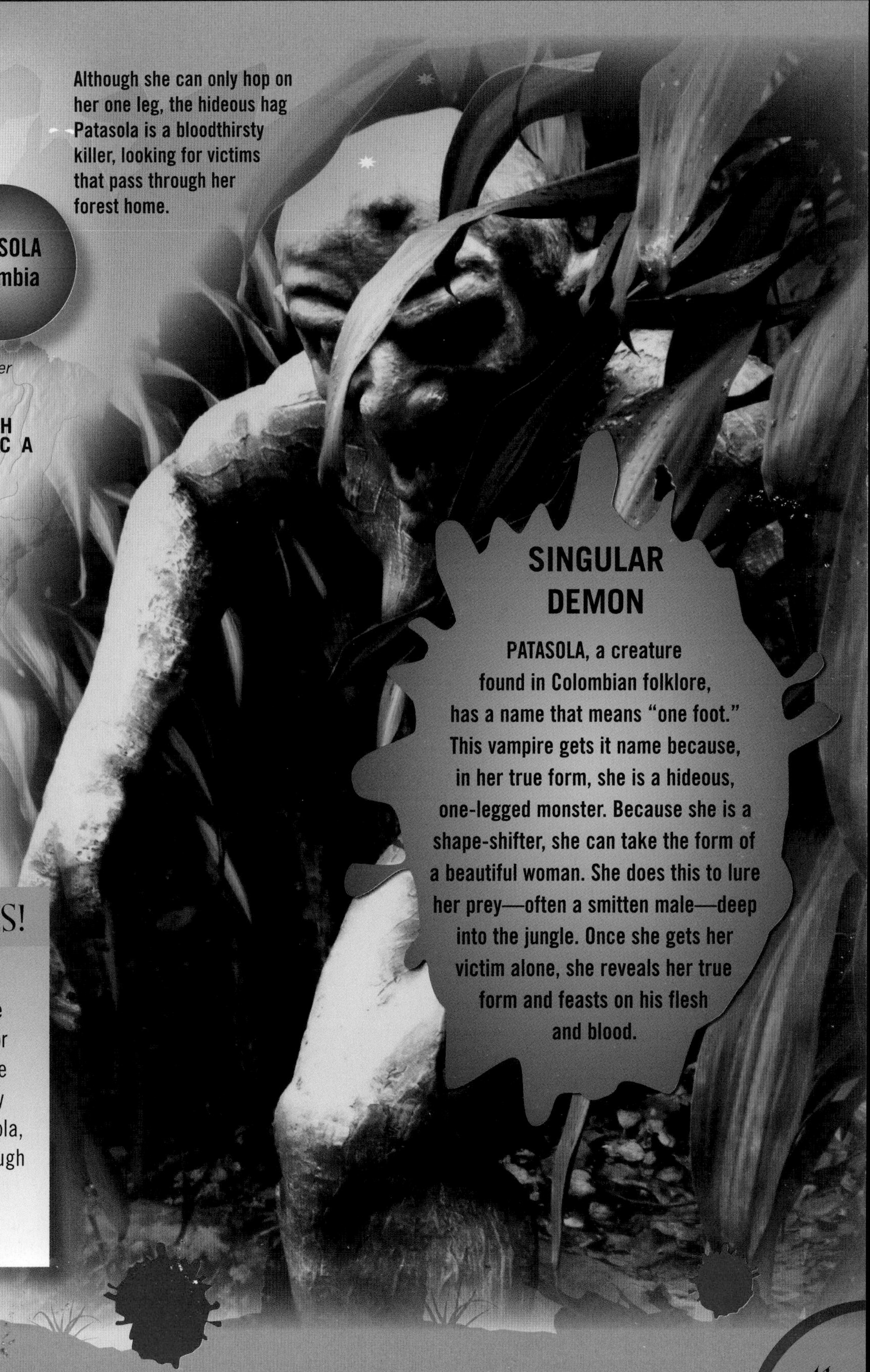

SINGULAR DEMON

PATASOLA, a creature found in Colombian folklore, has a name that means "one foot." This vampire gets it name because, in her true form, she is a hideous, one-legged monster. Because she is a shape-shifter, she can take the form of a beautiful woman. She does this to lure her prey—often a smitten male—deep into the jungle. Once she gets her victim alone, she reveals her true form and feasts on his flesh and blood.

WATCH OUT FOR THE HOOVES!

DEER WOMAN is a shape-shifter who appears in the myths of many American Indian peoples. She is said to take the shape of an old hag, a deer, or a young, lovely woman. In her beautiful form, she lures men to their deaths—unless they are lucky enough to notice her feet. Like Tunda and Patasola, her ability to shape-shift has a weakness. Although the rest of her can change, no matter what form she takes, she always has the hooves of a deer.

Vampires of Asia

Asia is a vast continent, so it isn't surprising to find out that its diverse peoples have a vast range of beliefs. But, despite the enormous range, just like everywhere else, there is no shortage of tales about bloodthirsty demons and ghouls.

Batgirl, Perhaps?

The *manananggal* is a female vampire from folklore of the Philippines. Although she has batlike wings, she is said to be beautiful. She kills her victims and drinks their blood. Like Eastern European vampires, she is vulnerable to garlic. Place garlic around the windows and doors of the house and the *manananggal* will stay away.

A carving of Rangda, queen of the Bali demons

THE BAD BREATH VAMPIRE!

THE *CHIANG-SHIH* is a vampire found in Chinese folklore. This vampire is considered one of the undead. A *chiang-shih* is an evil, reanimated corpse. It stalks its prey during the night, attacking its victims and draining their life force, as well as their blood. Its breath is said to be poisonous.

A Very Messy Vampire

The *leyak* is a vampire found in the folklore of Bali. This mythological creature can be either male or female. You can become a *leyak* though the use of black magic. *Leyaks* haunt graveyards and are shape-shifters that can transform themselves into animals or humans. They are said to have large fangs. During the day, *leyaks* look like regular people, but come nightfall, the head and entrails (internal organs) detach

Vampire-like demons appear in the folklore of many of the island nations of the Pacific Ocean.

CHINA

VIETNAM

SOUTH CHINA SEA

PHILIPPINES

PACIFIC OCEAN

THAILAND

Sulu Sea

Celebes Sea

MALAYSIA

INDONESIA

Java Sea

Bali Sea

INDIAN OCEAN

Bali

from the body. Without the extra weight, the *leyak* flies about looking for victims. The queen of the *leyaks* is called Rangda. Rangda is also queen of the demons.

A Nice Fresh Corpse

The *vetala*, or *baital*, is a vampire-like creature from the Hindu mythology of India. *Vetalas* are created when evil spirits inhabit fresh corpses of the newly dead. These creatures like to haunt cemeteries. They have a particular fondness for killing children. To destroy a *vetala*, one must separate the spirit from the body by performing very special burial rites.

OOZING VAMPS

THE *PENANGGAL* IS A MALAYSIAN vampire described as a beautiful woman. Like many vampires all over the world, the *penanggal* is a woman who has become a vampire through the use of black magic.

The *penanggal* has fangs, which she uses to pierce the flesh of her victims so that she can slurp up their blood. A chilling variation of the folklore concerning this vampire says that she can walk through walls and ooze through even the smallest cracks in the floorboards to get to her victims. To kill a *penanggal*, you must track it to her lair and burn the body.

VAMPIRE CHIC

PEOPLE IN BALI AND INDONESIA hang carvings of *leyaks* in their homes as decoration. These carvings proudly display the long tongue and oversized fangs of the *leyaks*.

A leyak mask hangs on display in a Balinese market.

Scratched to Death

The *rakshasa* also comes from India and is found in Hindu and Buddhist mythology. A female *rakshasa* is called a *rakshasi*. They are shape-shifters who can take human and animal form. They have venomous fingernails and fangs that they use to kill their victims. They are especially greedy, so they eat their victims' flesh, as well as drink their blood. These demons, like the vampires of Eastern Europe, are vulnerable to sunlight. Exorcism also destroys them.

A Heck of a Hangover

The goddess Kali, also known as Kalika, is a Hindu goddess associated with death and destruction. Her name means "the black one." She is often depicted with fangs and draped with the severed human heads of her victims. She is said to drink the blood of her enemies. On occasion, she drinks so much that she gets "drunk" on blood.

Vampiric Animals

Some animals use blood as their main source of food. The mosquito is a tiny version of a blood-sucking critter, but there are other creatures, larger and more dangerous. One is the vampire bat.

A vampire bat has a distinctive, upturned snout.

MEXICO

Gulf of Mexico

ATLANTIC OCEAN

Caribbean Sea

Central America

SOUTH AMERICA

PACIFIC OCEAN

Vampiric mosquitoes are always females. In order to provide enough protein to feed the eggs developing inside of them, mosquito moms feed on blood. Their tubelike mouths have serrated edges that slice into skin.

Bats, Bats, Bats

There are three species of vampire bat: the common vampire bat (*Desmodus rotundus*), the hairy-legged vampire bat (*Diphylla ecaudata*), and the white-winged vampire bat (*Diaemus youngi*). All three species live in the Americas. The vampire bat can be found drinking blood from Mexico to Brazil, and in Chile and Argentina. Like human vampires of folklore, vampire bats feed when darkness falls. And

The brown-shaded area in the map, left, shows the range of the common vampire bat.

WHAT'S IN A NAME?

VAMPIRE BATS are named after human vampires—and not the other way around. European explorers in South America noticed that some of the local bats and the vampires of legend had something in common: the feeding habits!

LIFTOFF

A vampire bat consumes so much blood, that in order to take off, it must first urinate and expel a large amount of urine. Then, when it is lighter, it crouches and flings its body into the air.

DID YOU KNOW?

Vampire bats live in dark places, such as hollow trees, caves, old wells, and even the attics of people's houses!

A common vampire bat hangs upside down in its cave. It tucks its wings close to its body.

when it comes time to eat, the common vampire bat feeds almost exclusively on mammals. And humans, wouldn't you know, are mammals!

The Better to Hear You With

The vampire bat has special sensors that allow it to sense its victim's blood. Its hearing is also adapted to hear the sound of its prey sleeping. It will often stalk its prey on the ground, too, because this bat can walk and even run after its prey.

The Better to Drink You With

The vampire bat's front teeth, like the human vampire's teeth, are super sharp and perfect for cutting into flesh. Once the bat has inflicted its wound, it laps up the blood with its tongue. The vampire bat's teeth inject its saliva into the victim when the bat bites. The saliva contains a special substance called draculin (named after the count) that prevents the victim's blood from clotting. Now, the vampire bat can drink at its leisure.

A Shave and a Haircut

The vampire bat uses its sharp teeth to shave the fur or hair off its victim. Its incisor and cheek teeth act like a razor. The bat can then attack the vulnerable, naked flesh below.

Not Just Bats

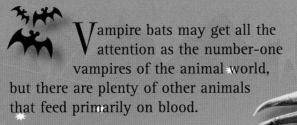

Vampire bats may get all the attention as the number-one vampires of the animal world, but there are plenty of other animals that feed primarily on blood.

Ticks

Ticks are eight-legged bugs that live on the blood of mammals, birds, and even a few reptiles and amphibians. They often live in tall grasses and shrubs, where they will wait to find and then attach themselves to passing hosts.

Vampire finches

Blue-footed and red-footed boobies, and their cousins the masked boobies, have to beware. These birds live on the Galápagos Islands in the Pacific Ocean off Ecuador, but it's no island paradise. Little vampire finches sometimes take their meals by pecking on the boobies' hindquarters until they bleed. After one of them makes the initial cut, its flock mates all line up to take turns sipping up the blood!

Leeches

There are many varieties of leeches, but all of them feast on blood. For centuries, medical wisdom held that "bleeding" an ill person allowed toxins to escape the body. Today, doctors around the world still use leeches to help thin patients' blood.

The medicinal leech, *Hirudo medicinalis*, is used to draw blood from human patients.

Above, an electron microscope image of a minuscule flea. Your family pet may prefer a bite from one vampire than an assault from hundreds of these biting bloodsuckers.

It may be more than twice the size of a vampire finch, but the red-footed booby, shown above, has to watch out for the smaller bird's vampiric habits.

THE GOAT SUCKER

ALTHOUGH SOME PEOPLE claim to have seen the *chupacabra* with their own eyes, this blood-drinking animal most likely exists only in legend. *Chupacabra* (which translates as "goat sucker") gets its name because it is rumored to attack and drink the blood of animals, particularly goats. Tales of the *chupacabra* can be found in Puerto Rico, Mexico, and Latin American communities in the United States. This creature has been described as reptilian in appearance with scaly, greenish skin, and eyes that glow red in the dark.

Candiru Catfish

These little catfish (only about 1 inch long) live in South America's Amazon and Orinoco Rivers, where they suck up blood from the gills of other fish. Swimmers beware! These hungry little catfish also like to invade human orifices looking for meals!

Fleas

There are thousands of species of this tiny insect, and all of them feed on the blood of mammals and birds.

Bedbugs

These minuscule creatures are the pesky nuisances that live in soft spots like mattresses, where they can easily draw a meal from a sleeping human.

Oxpecker

Famous as the birds that live aboard the backs of African rhinoceroses, water buffaloes, and other large mammals, oxpeckers not only remove parasites from their hosts, they also sip their blood!

KEEP IT SIMPLE

IN 2005, A TEAM FILMING the BBC TV series *Amazon Abyss* discovered a new species of aquatic bloodsucker in the Amazon River. Scientists had no trouble coming up with its common name, "vampire fish," but decided to leave its scientific name to a vote. They held a poll on the BBC Web site, asking Web users to decide. Voters passed on the following choices:

- *Paracanthopoma draculae.* "Draculae" comes from Bram Stoker's *Dracula.*

- *Paracanthopoma irritans.* "Irritans" is part of the scientific name for the flea—the scientists figured that this bloodthirsty little fish is as annoying as a flea.

- *Paracanthopoma minuta.* "Minuta" suggests just how small this fish is.

- *Paracanthopoma nosferatu.* "Nosferatu" was the name of the earliest film version of Dracula, the 1922 silent film *Nosferatu.*

And the winner is . . . *Paracanthopoma vampyra*, or simply, "vampire fish."

Yellow-beaked oxpeckers, shown below perching on a water buffalo, feast on parasites such as ticks that feed on their hosts' blood. Oxpeckers do more good than harm but sometimes they drink blood directly from open wounds on the hosts' backs.

Vampires in Modern Times

Today, tales of vampires can be found all over the world. But unlike vampires in days of yore, modern vamps are not always considered revolting monsters. Vampires are now often depicted as seductive, alluring, charismatic, and even romantic. Although they are still viewed as dangerous, this air of danger has become part of their appeal. Books and movies about vampires often portray them as capable of both good and evil. Rather than being feared, vampires can now be understood—and sometimes even loved. No longer cadaverous, hideous, and dreadful, the vampires of today are beautiful—aglow with the vigor of undead health. And unlike other supernatural creatures, modern vampires are so seductive that many would willingly join their undead ranks. Power, beauty, and immortality—who *wouldn't* want to be a vampire?

Literary Vampires

Early portrayals of vampires in literature were usually of corpselike creatures, who were pale, thin, hideous, and vicious. In the novel *Dracula*, for example, the count is described as a towering, cadaverous old man. Once Dracula arrived on the big screen, however, he was portrayed as suave, smooth, debonair, and irresistible. On occasion, he was even portrayed as aristocratic, tragic, and lonely.

Romantic Vamps

Novelists took their cue from these romanticized portraits of vampires and expanded on it. Today, vampires in literature are almost universally beautiful and seductive. And if a vampire has a hideous side, he also has a seductive side that he shows to the world.

A headstone nearly falls over in one of the old sections of Highgate Cemetery.

THE HIGHGATE VAMPIRE

HIGHGATE CEMETERY IN LONDON opened for business in 1839. By 1975, it was so dilapidated that parts of the cemetery were closed to the public—but not before it had acquired a reputation for occult activity. In February 1970, the *Hampstead and Highgate Express*, a local newspaper, printed a story about a vampire rumored to be roaming the overgrown paths of Highgate Cemetery. According to the story, this vampire was a medieval nobleman from Eastern Europe who had dabbled in black magic during his lifetime. For some reason, he had been buried in London on the site that would later become the cemetery. After the story appeared in the newspapers, so-called vampire hunters swarmed Highgate Cemetery, eager to slay the Highgate Vampire. Things got so out of hand that the police had to be called in to get matters under control.

An urn marks an unkempt grave in a wooded area of Highgate Cemetery. It's not hard to believe that the undead walk in this spooky landscape.

JET-SETTING VAMPIRE

HORROR AUTHOR STEPHEN KING wrote *'Salem's Lot*. The novel is about a town infested with young vampires. It was made into a TV miniseries twice; once in 1979 and again in 2004. Like *'Salem's Lot*, Stephen King's short story "The Night Flier" was also made into a film. "Night Flier" tells the chilling story of a reporter hot on the trail of a vampire who travels by private plane. The plane lands at night at small isolated airports, and the vampire feeds on the locals.

SOUTHERN-FRIED VAMPIRES

AN ADULT VAMPIRE SERIES written by Anne Rice and set in New Orleans chronicles the adventures of a French vampire named Lestat. The first and third of these books were made into movies. *Interview with the Vampire*, starring Brad Pitt, Tom Cruise, Antonio Banderas, and Kirsten Dunst, was released in 1994. *Queen of the Damned*, starring Aaliyah and Stuart Townsend, was released in 2002. The vampires in these novels are always beautiful, sometimes melancholy, and often lonely.

Early Books

Dracula was not the first novel published about vampires. In 1819, John Polidori published a novella, or short novel, called *The Vampyre*. It was a great success. And in 1847, James Malcolm Rymer published the book *Varney the Vampire: or The Feast of Blood*. This also proved popular. Finally, in 1871, Sheridan Le Fanu published the novella *Carmilla*. This novella, along with *Varney the Vampire*, had a big influence on Bram Stoker's work.

Sheridan Le Fanu

Brad Pitt as the vampire Louis in the movie version of the book *The Vampire Lestat*

A PENNY FOR YOUR THOUGHTS

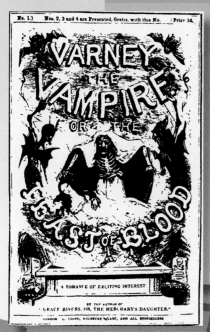

THE PUBLISHERS called *Varney the Vampire, or the Feast of Blood*, "a romance of exciting interest" and published it in installments. This type of book was known as a "penny dreadful." Penny dreadfuls were usually sensational stories, which were sold by the chapter for a penny apiece. These stories, aimed at teenagers, featured gruesome contents and dramatic illustrations.

Title page from *Varney the Vampire*

The Twilight Vampires

The Twilight series of novels by Stephanie Meyer takes the vampire legend to a new level. The first novel in the four-book series, *Twilight*, tells the story of Isabella "Bella" Swan, a teenaged girl who falls in love with Edward Cullen, a 107-year-old vampire, who she meets in high school. Edward is handsome, compelling, and eternally 17 years old. He lives with a family of "vegetarian" vampires that includes Carlisle, Esme, Rosalie, Emmett, Jasper, and Alice. The vampires in Stephanie Meyer's novels are most unusual. Not only are they beautiful, but they are also immortal, can go out in the daytime, choose between good and evil, and even have children.

UPPER-CRUST VAMPIRES

The town of Volterra, in the Tuscany region of Italy, is the fictional home of the Volturi. The Volturi are a coven of ancient vampires, who are considered vampire royalty by younger vampires. In *New Moon*, the second book in the Twilight series, the Volturi live beneath the city and collect their victims from the visiting tourists above. Not all vampires, unfortunately, are vegetarians like the Cullens!

Although vampire Edward Cullen has lived for more than a century, he never found a soulmate until he met Bella Swan.

In *Twilight*, Edward lives with a coven of vampires known as the Cullen family. They survive by drinking the blood of animals rather than killing humans for their blood. Above, the Cullen family shares a cafeteria table. From left to right: Jasper Hale and his wife, Alice Cullen; Emmet Cullen; Rosalie Hale; and Edward.

ANCIENT WEREWOLF LEGENDS

ALONG WITH VAMPIRES, the Twilight series also features werewolves, or shape-shifters. Some of the characters can change their shapes at will into that of large wolves. La Push, Washington, is home to the Quileute Tribal Reservation in the books, as well as in real life. A tribal legend says that long ago supernatural forces created the Quileute peoples from wolves. Stephanie Meyer uses this legend as the basis for her version of werewolf folklore. In *New Moon*, Bella's friend Jacob Black, a member of the Quileute, transforms into a werewolf.

RAIN + MIST = VAMPIRES

IN REAL LIFE, THE TOWN of Forks, Washington, where the character Bella lives with her father, is known for its frequent rainfall. The town is located in the heart of the Olympic Peninsula between the Olympic Mountains and ocean beaches. Forks High School, which Bella attends, is located at 261 Spartan Avenue. The town of Forks is named after the nearby rivers. Its nickname is the "logging capital of the world." Chilly and rainy year round, the average high temperature in June is 63 degrees and the average low is 46. The frequent cloud cover makes this town a perfect place for sunlight-avoiding vampires to reside.

Quileute Tribal Reservation, a real location used in the fictional Twilight series, is the westernmost Indian reservation in the continental United States.

Forks
La Push
Quileute Tribal Reservation
Seattle
Washington
PACIFIC OCEAN
Portland
Oregon

Not all of the vampires living in Forks are as benign as Edward and his family. Above, James (left), a "tracker" vampire who kills for fun, surveys the scene with his coven members Laurent (center) and Victoria.

The damp and dreary weather of Bella's home of Forks, Washington, is well suited to a vampire's need to stay out of the bright sun.

TWILIGHT, THE MOVIE

THE MOVIE VERSION OF *TWILIGHT* stars Kirsten Stewart as Bella Swan and Robert Pattinson as Edward Cullen. Many of the scenes were shot in Portland, Oregon, rather than in Forks, Washington. The movie's producers plan to turn all four books in the Twilight series into feature films.

Vampires on the Big Screen

Since the early days of film, vampires have been compelling subjects for filmmakers. The portrayal of vampires on the big screen ranges from hideous and evil to beautiful and heroic.

No longer are vampire movies just scary. Today, they are funny, romantic, and exciting. But notwithstanding all the new vampires, the original movie vampire and most well-known vampire of all is, and always will be, Count Dracula.

Kiefer Sutherland as the "head" vampire in *The Lost Boys*

LOOK OUT!

The tag line from the release of the original *Dracula* movie was, "The story of the strangest passion the world has ever known!" The tag line from *Dracula's Daughter* was, "Look out, she'll get you!" *Dracula's Daughter*, released in 1936, is considered a sequel to *Dracula*.

Roddy McDowell plays a vampire killer in *Fright Night*.

CLASSIC MOVIES

THERE ARE HUNDREDS of vampire films, but a few stand out as classic scary movies.

- *Dracula* (1931), starring Bela Lugosi
- *The Hunger* (1983), starring Catherine Deneuve, David Bowie, and Susan Sarandon
- *Fright Night* (1985), starring Chris Sarandon and Roddy McDowell
- *The Lost Boys* (1987), Corey Haim, Kiefer Sutherland, and Corey Feldman
- *Bram Stoker's Dracula* (1992), starring Gary Oldman, Winona Ryder, Keanu Reeves, and Anthony Hopkins

MOVIES OF NOTE

- *Underworld* (2003)
- *Blade* (1998)
- *Queen of the Damned* (2002)
- *Near Dark* (1987)
- *From Dusk till Dawn* (1996)

Bela Lugosi as the count in the 1931 version of *Dracula*

DID YOU KNOW?

Count Dracula is second only to the famous detective Sherlock Holmes as the fictional character most often depicted in feature films.

Gary Oldman as Dracula in *Bram Stoker's Dracula*

Above, Kate Beckinsale as a warrior vampire and, left, Michael Sheen as one of the enemy Lycans, or werewolves, in *Underworld*

Nosferatu poster from 1922

Nosferatu

The first film version of Bram Stoker's *Dracula* was a German movie called *Nosferatu*. This silent film portrays Count Dracula as a ghastly creature with bat-like ears, ratlike teeth, and unnaturally long fingers. In fact, the makeup department intentionally lengthened the actor's fingers as the film went on. Because Stoker's widow would not give the filmmakers permission to use the book, they had to alter some things from the novel. For instance, they changed Dracula's name to Count Orlock.

Above, Klaus Kinski plays Count Orlock in the 1979 version of Nosferatu.

Left, Max Schreck in the original *Nosferatu*. Unlike the debonair nobleman of later films, *Nosferatu* depicts the lead vampire as a creepy ghoul.

DID YOU KNOW?

The title *Nosferatu* comes from the Greek word meaning "plague-carrier." The word was used by Bram Stoker in his novel and later became a popular way to refer to vampires in fictional literature.

In *Blacula*, William Marshall played an African prince whose run-in with Count Dracula turns him into a vampire.

OFFBEAT MOVIES

- *Blacula* (1972)—a cult classic
- *Lifeforce* (1985)—extraterrestrial vampires invade Earth
- *Vampire in Brooklyn* (1995)—Eddie Murphy as an urban vampire
- *Dracula: Dead and Loving It* (1995)—Dracula as a comedy
- *Dracula 3000* (2004)—Dracula in outer space

DID YOU KNOW?

During the 1970s, vampires were so popular that a breakfast cereal named Count Chocula was created.

Leslie Nielson played the count in *Dracula: Dead and Loving It*, a comedy spoof of scary vampire movies.

IN THE FLESH

MANY ACTORS have played the role of Dracula in the movies and on stage. Here are a few of the most famous:

- Bela Lugosi
- Christopher Lee
- Frank Langella
- Raul Julia
- Gary Oldman

Christopher Lee, at 6 feet, 5 inches, is the tallest screen Dracula, a role he played in 10 films.

Bela Lugosi, the star of the original authorized film version of *Dracula*, was born Béla Ferenc Dezso Blaskó in the land of vampires: Lugos, Austria–Hungary, which is now known as Lugoj, Romania. Lugosi was a successful actor in his home country before he moved to the United States and eventually starred in a movie that would forever connect him to vampire lore.

The Real Dracula

Universal Studios in Hollywood, California, didn't take much time in getting their version of *Dracula* in theaters. They began filming on September 29, 1930, and were done on November 15. Moviegoers first saw it February 12, 1931. The movie was a huge hit and became the top moneymaker of the year.

DID YOU KNOW?

During the filming of the Spanish-language version of *Dracula*, which was filmed at the same time as the American version, the budget was so tight that the actor who played Dracula wore Bela Lugosi's hairpiece!

Helen Chandler played Mina Harker, the count's tragic victim in *Dracula*.

Bela Lugosi's portrayal of the vampire in white tie and tails set the standard for Draculas to come.

DOUBLE DRACULA

BELA LUGOSI PLAYED MANY vampires in his movie career, but he played the role of Count Dracula only twice: once in the movie *Dracula*, and once as the head vamp himself in the comedy *Abbott and Costello Meet Frankenstein*.

A HANDSOME VAMPIRE

BELA LUGOSI REFUSED the role of Frankenstein because he didn't want to wear so much makeup. He wanted his handsome face to be recognizable in the role. In addition, he objected to the dialogue, which was nothing but a series of grunts and groans. The part went to Boris Karloff, and the rest was history.

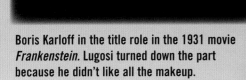

Boris Karloff in the title role in the 1931 movie *Frankenstein.* Lugosi turned down the part because he didn't like all the makeup.

In 1948, Lugosi played the vampire for laughs in the comedy *Abbott and Costello Meet Frankenstein.*

"I *Vant* to Suck Your Blood . . ."
Lugosi did not speak English very well when he was cast in the role of the Transylvanian count. The director had to give him instructions in French, which Lugosi spoke. He learned his lines phonetically, memorizing them by sound. This is why he speaks so strangely in the movie. He also had a thick Hungarian accent.

A Role of a Lifetime
Lugosi died in bed while reading a script called "The Final Curtain." For his funeral, Lugosi was dressed in his Dracula outfit for the open-casket viewing. He was wearing a tuxedo, a cape, and his vampire makeup!

DID YOU KNOW?
As well as *Dracula*, Universal Studios also produced the horror classics *The Wolfman, The Mummy*, and *Frankenstein.*

Small-Screen Vampires

Vampires show up in many TV series, from comic characters on Halloween episodes of weekly series, such as *The Simpsons*, to dramatic miniseries and movies that tell darker tales of our favorite demons.

Just Your Normal Family

In the 1950s and 1960s, there were lots of TV comedies about "average" families with Mom, Dad, and the kids. In 1964, a new TV family became a big hit—but it was not your average family. Although the Munsters acted as if they were just like everyone else, they were . . . well . . . a bit different.

In fact, the dad, Herman, was a Frankenstein look-alike, the mom, Lily, resembled Dracula's daughter (which was not surprising considering that her father, Grandpa, was a dead ringer for an aging Count Dracula), and their son, Eddie, was a young werewolf. Only poor cousin Marilyn—who by Munsters' standards is unfortunately ugly—is the only normal human living at 1313 Mockingbird Lane.

Made-for-TV Vampires

Vampires have made it into a few made-for-TV movies, including the 1977 film *Count Dracula*, which closely followed the plot of Bram Stoker's novel. In 1972, *The Night Stalker* became the highest-ranked TV movie up until that time. It was so successful that it became a weekly show.

TOP 5: TV VAMPS

1. **Barnabas Collins** in *Dark Shadows*, played by Jonathan Frid, 1966–1971
2. **Angel** in *Angel* and *Buffy*, played by David Boreanaz, 1997–2004
3. **Grandpa** in *The Munsters*, played by Al Lewis, 1964–1966
4. **Nick Knight** in *Forever Knight,* played by Geraint Wyn Davies, 1992–1996
5. **Bill Compton** in *True Blood*, played by Stephen Moyer, 2008–present

The Munsters: not just-your-average suburban family. From left: Eddie, Lily, Marilyn, and Grandpa, with Herman standing at rear.

Twenty-First-Century Vampires

With the success of shows like *Buffy* and *Angel*, even more TV shows picked up the vampire theme. In Canada, *Vampire High* featured a boarding school for humans that started accepting teen vamps in the hope of "civilizing" them. In Japan, the anime series tells the story of *The Vampire Knight*. In the United States, vampires popped up more than once on the occult-themed hit *The X-Files* and on *Supernatural*. There was also the crime-fighting vampire Mick St. John of *Moonlight* and demon-fighting reporter Carl Kolchak in *The Night Stalker* (a remake of the 1970s series). Another popular series of books, the Sookie Stackhouse series by Charlaine Harris, has been turned into a TV show. *True Blood* is about how humans and vampires coexist in a small Louisiana town after the development of synthetic blood allows vamps to live normal lives.

Anna Paquin plays Sookie Stackhouse, a mind-reading mortal with a crush on vampire Bill Compton, played by Stephen Moyer, in the TV series *True Blood*.

BLOOD IN THE AFTERNOON

ONE OF THE MOST MEMORABLE of all TV vampires is Barnabas Collins of the Gothic soap opera *Dark Shadows*. This spooky daytime serial featured Barnabas, the 200-year-old blood drinker, but also a cast of witches, werewolves, warlocks, zombies, ghosts, and even a Frankenstein-like monster.

Jonathan Frid played vampire Barnabas Collins in TV's only horror soap opera, *Dark Shadows*.

An Unlikely Slayer

Before 1992, if you thought "vampire slayer," you probably thought of a big, bad tough guy. That stereotype changed forever when California high school cheerleader Buffy Summers finds out that she is her generation's Chosen One. She goes from being an airhead blonde to humanity's protector from vampires, demons, and the forces of darkness.

The Two Buffys

Before Buffy came to television, *Buffy the Vampire Slayer* was a feature film. Released in 1992, it starred Kristy Swanson as Buffy. The television series was introduced in 1997 and continued until 2003. The show was about an ordinary teenage girl, who had supernatural abilities and was chosen by fate to battle vampires and the forces of evil. Sarah Michelle Geller played Buffy.

Sarah Michelle Geller, right, as TV's *Buffy the Vampire Slayer*, vanquishes a demon.

Poster for the movie version of *Buffy the Vampire Slayer*

David Boreanaz as the brooding vampire Angel

ANGELS AND DEMONS

BUFFY VIEWERS found the character Angel so appealing that this vampire-with-a-heart got his own show. *Angel*, starring David Boreanaz, followed the adventures of the 200-year-old vampire whose soul was returned to him by Gypsies. The once-bloodthirsty fiend gives up killing for sport and dedicates his life to "helping the helpless." This means that he and his comrades—including humans and other demons-gone-good—must every week battle an assortment of monsters and ghouls who threaten innocent humans.

James Marsters as Spike. Spike was supposed to be killed off during *Buffy*'s second season. His character proved to be so popular that the platinum-haired vampire stuck around Sunnydale.

The Making of *Buffy*

Scenes from the movie and television series were shot in and around Los Angeles, California. Scenes in Sunnydale High School, featured in the television series, were shot at Torrance High School in Torrance, California. The fictional University of California, at Sunnydale, featured in the fourth season of *Buffy*, was shot at the University of California, Los Angeles (UCLA) campus in Westwood, and at California State University. Exterior shots of Buffy's house were shot at a real house in Torrance, California.

TORRANCE
Torrance High School served as the setting for Sunnydale High. *Buffy* also used a real house in Torrance as the exterior of the Summers house.

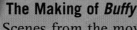

California

Torrance

Los Angeles

LOS ANGELES
UCLA's Westwood campus stood in for *Buffy*'s fictional Sunnydale campus.

PUNK-ROCK VAMP

SPIKE FIRST APPEARED ON *BUFFY* as a villainous vampire. Eventually, he falls in love with Buffy and regains his soul. Spike later moved to the show *Angel*, where he reluctantly joins up with his former enemy to vanquish evil.

The "Scooby Gang"

Even the Chosen One needs friends—and a little help with the slaying duties. Her best friends, Willow and Xander, and popular-girl competitor, Cordelia, along with others, join Buffy in her quest to keep the world safe from the supernatural. They call themselves the Scooby Gang, after the ghost-hunting teens on the cartoon series *Scooby-Doo*.

Buffy (Sarah Michelle Geller), center, with Xander (Nicholas Brendon), Willow (Alyson Hannigan), left, and Cordelia (Charisma Carpenter), right, members of the Scooby Gang. Like other *Buffy* characters, Cordelia moved to the spin-off show *Angel*.

The Folklore of Vampires

Vampires, among all supernatural creatures, are some of the most seductive and alluring. Not many people would want to become a werewolf, mummy, or witch.

Vampires, though, called "the children of the night," hold a special fascination for most of us. But how do you become a vampire? And is there a cure for vampirism? If you came across an evil vampire rather than a noble, vegetarian vampire, how do you protect yourself? Can a vampire be killed—again? How do you even recognize a vampire?

These are very good questions. And in order to answer them, you need to explore the folklore of vampires.

Vampires can take many forms, and they can often change appearance. One minute they can be beautiful, and the next, they look like hideous fang-baring demons.

A VAMPIRE Q&A

What are a vampire's habitats?

Vampires prefer secluded, lonely locations. Abandoned houses, caves, crypts in cemeteries, and tunnels are a few of a vampire's preferred hiding spots. Vampires need darkness, so their lairs will usually be windowless or boarded up. In olden times, vampires lived more lavishly in castles, manors, or stone towers.

Avoid abandoned houses in out-of-the-way places. Vampires may be using it as their lair!

What are a vampire's powers?

- Immortality
- Superhuman strength
- Invulnerability and rapid healing
- Ability to shape-shift into a wolf, bat, or mist
- Mind control through telepathic or hypnotic powers
- Ability to command animals
- Ability to fly or levitate
- Ability to create and then control fledging vampires
- Enhanced senses
- Enhanced beauty

Because they are undead, vampires do not need air. Consequently, vampires can travel underwater, survive underground, survive being buried alive, and survive being sealed in crypts. Some would consider this a weakness, because a vampire can be entombed alive for all eternity. And eternity, as we all know, is an awfully long time.

Wolfsbane, *Aconitum variegatum*, is known to weaken vampires. It's also called monkshood because the purple flowers are shaped like the hood of a monk's robe.

Garlic: not so great for your breath, but very effective in warding off vampires

What are a vampire's weaknesses?

- Inability to cross running water
- Vulnerable to sunlight
- No reflection
- Vulnerable to holy objects, such as crosses, holy water, and communion wafers
- Vulnerable to garlic
- Vulnerable to wolfsbane
- Must sleep during the day
- Cannot enter a dwelling unless invited
- Must rest in the soil of its birthplace.

Many vampires are repulsed by the sight of a crucifix, or cross.

How do you protect yourself from a vampire?

- Wear a cross at all times.
- Wear a wreath of garlic.
- Stay away from known vampire haunts, such as cemeteries and abandoned houses.
- Don't invite a vampire into your house.
- Many vampires like to hunt in packs, so beware of locations where vampires are prone to congregate at night—like dark forests and dense woods.

This vampire is as good as dead. Nailing it into its coffin destroys a vampire permanently.

How do you become a vampire?

The main way is by being bitten by a vampire. One theory is that the bite of vampire deposits a type of virus that spreads through the victim's body, destroying the victim's human blood and replacing it with vampiric blood. The human turns into a vampire when all human systems become vampiric.

Another theory is that the vampire drains the victim's blood and kills the victim, allowing a demon to inhabit the victim's body. The recently transformed vampire may remember its human existence, but it is no longer human. The fledgling vampire now has the dark desires of a demon.

What is the best way to hunt a vampire?

Because vampire hunters can no longer be hired to do the job, vampires must be hunted very carefully. Be prepared for all contingencies. Take trusted friends along. Begin the hunt early in the day so that there is sufficient daylight for protection. Finally, be prepared to run very quickly and scream for help.

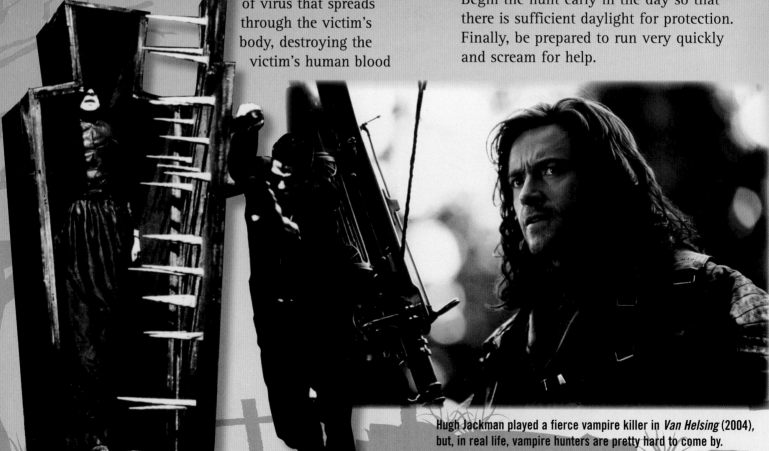

Hugh Jackman played a fierce vampire killer in *Van Helsing* (2004), but, in real life, vampire hunters are pretty hard to come by.

How do you kill a vampire?

- Drive a wooden stake through the heart.
- Decapitate it.
- Burn it with fire.
- Expose it to sunlight.
- Nail the body inside its coffin.
- Dismember it.

What happens to a vampire's body once the vampire is destroyed?

Sunlight can cause a vampire to burn up completely, turning it into fine ash. Similarly, a wooden stake driven through the heart can cause a vampire to instantly turn to dust, or quickly decay and be reduced to a pile of greasy clothes.

Vampires can stand a few seconds of exposure to sunlight, but eventually, the rays will ignite them, leaving just ashes behind.

Hammering a wooden stake through the heart of a vampire is one of the ways to kill them.

FINAL WORD

VAMPIRES, WHETHER THEY are charismatic and sophisticated, or hideous and evil, are the most appealing monsters of all. Neither alive nor dead, neither inherently good nor born evil, vampires appeal to the desire in all of us for immortality and freedom from society's rules. When one becomes a vampire, one leaves the daytime world behind, along with its tedious responsibilities and chafing rules. It is perhaps strange that vampires, once so feared, have evolved into an appealing mystery. But appeal they do—to the romantic in all of us and to our desire to experience the dark side of humanity. Vampires are here to stay.

Find Out More

DEMONS TO AVOID

adze (pronounced ODD-zee). African vampire-like creature that can turn into a firefly

baobhan sith (pronounced BAA-van shee). Beautiful but bloodthirsty Scottish fairy creature with deer hooves for feet

Camazotz (pronounced CA-ma-zotz). Maya bat god

chiang-shih (pronounced schong-SHE). Reanimated corpse from Chinese folklore

chupacabra (pronounced CHEW-pa-CA-bra). Scaly, blood-drinking creature from Spanish folklore

dhampir (pronounced HAHM-peer). The offspring of a vampire and a human

djinn (pronounced JIN). Demon, also known as a genie, from Arabic folklore

edimmu (pronounced ED-ee-moo). Blood-drinking Sumerian demon. Also known as an *ekimmu*

Empusa (pronounced em-POO-SA). Shape-shifting demon from ancient Greek mythology, and daughter of Hecate, the goddess of witchcraft

estrie (pronounced es-TREE). Witchy demon from Hebrew folklore

gallu (pronounced GAH-loo). Mesopotamian demon and kidnapper of children

Kali (pronounced KAH-lee). Fanged-toothed Hindu goddess

keres (pronounced KEE-reez). Bloodthirsty death spirits from Greek mythology. Also called *ceres*

Lamashtu (pronounced LA-mosh-too). Daughter of Babylonian sky god Anu; terrible demon that kidnapped children

Lamia (pronounced La-ME-a). A child-murdering demon; half woman and half serpent

leanan sídhe (pronounced LAN-awn-shee). Beautiful but deadly fairy woman from Irish folklore

leyak (pronounced LAY-ak). Deadly, fanged vampire of Bali

liannan shith (pronounced LAN-awn-shee). Beautiful but deadly dancing fairy from Scottish folklore

Lilith (pronounced LIL-ith). Beautiful but deadly queen of the demons in Hebrew and Mesopotamian folklore

loogaroo (pronounced loo-GA-roo). Caribbean vampire that had made a pact with the Devil

manananggal (pronounced MA-na-nang-GAL). Beautiful, winged vampire from the Philippines

moroi (pronounced MO-roy). Romanian vampire

mullo (pronounced Moo-LOW). Revenge-seeking vampire from Romany, or Gypsy, folklore

Patasola (pronounced PA-ta-SO-la). Hideous, one-legged South American vampire

penanggal (pronounced PEN-ang-GAL). Witchy Malaysian vampire

peuchen (pronounced PEW-ken). Flying, snakelike South American vampire

rakshasa (pronounced ROCK-sha-sa). Flesh-eating demon in Hindu and Buddhist mythology

sasabonsam (pronounced sa-sa-BON-som). Iron-toothed, hook-footed African vampire

Sekhmet (pronounced SEK-met). Egyptian lion-headed goddess with a thirst for blood

shades (pronounced SHADES). Ghost-like demons mentioned in the ancient Greek epic *The Odyssey* by Homer

soucouyant (pronounced soo-COO-yan). Witchy vampire from Trinidad

striga (pronounced STREE-ga). Vampire-like demon from Roman mythology

strigoi (pronounced STREE-goy). Romanian vampire

strzyga (pronounced STREE-zy-gah). Polish vampire

Tunda (pronounced TOON-da). Flesh-loving South American vampire. Also called *La Tunda*

varkolak (pronounced var-KO-lack). Shape-shifting Bulgarian vampire

vetala (pronounced VEE-ta-la). Grave-haunting Hindu vampire-like demon. Also known as *baital*

vrykolakas (pronounced VREE-ko-la-kus). Door-knocking vampire from Greek folklore

WORDS TO KNOW

Akkad. Capital of the ancient Akkadian empire (2300 BCE–2100 BCE) of Mesopotamia, located where the Euphrates and Tigris Rivers are at their closest, near today's Baghdad, Iraq

amulet. A charm often inscribed with a magic incantation or symbol to protect against evil

Ashanti. A member of a people of southern Ghana in Western Africa

Assyria. An ancient civilization (1900 BC–612 BC) located in north Mesopotamia

Babylonia. An ancient civilization (2000 BC–539 BC) located in north Mesopotamia

black magic. A form of magic that draws on evil powers

boyar. A member of an aristocratic order next in rank below the ruling prince, once found in Russia, Wallachia, and other Eastern European countries

cadaverous. Resembling a corpse

cauldron. A large kettle used over open fires; used by evil fairies and witches

Celts. A group of peoples that occupied lands stretching from the British Isles to what is now Turkey

charlatan. One who pretends to know something. Fake vampire hunters were given this name in Eastern Europe.

communion wafer. A wafer used in Christian rites to symbolize the body of Christ; said to repel vampires

consecrate. To dedicate to a sacred purpose, such as a cemetery

dead ringer. Someone or something that is nearly identical to another

debonair. Gracious and sophisticated

decapitation. The chopping off of a head

demon. An evil spirit, or something that causes harm, distress, or ruin

demonology. The study of demons

draculin. A protein found in bat saliva that keeps blood from coagulating.

Eastern Europe. The easternmost area of Europe that includes the present-day nations of Albania, Belarus, Bosnia and Herzegovina, Bulgaria, Croatia, Cyprus, Czech Republic, Estonia, Greece, Hungary, Kosovo, Latvia, Lithuania, Macedonia, Malta, Moldova, Montenegro, Poland, Romania, Russia, Serbia, Slovakia, Slovenia, Turkey, and Ukraine

electron microscope. A type of microscope that uses electrons to illuminate a specimen and create a greatly enlarged image

elixir. A concoction or potion thought to have medicinal qualities

entrails. Internal organs, such as the intestines and liver

Ewe people. A group of peoples that live in the West African countries of Ghana, Togo, and Benin

exorcism. The act of expelling an evil spirit; usually performed by priests, shamans, and other people of high spiritual rank

fledgling. An inexperienced person who is learning a particular skill

ghoul. An evil being that robs graves and feeds on corpses

Gypsy. See *Romany*.

holy water. Water that has been blessed by a priest; used in religious rites; said to repel vampires

impalement. Killing someone by piercing them through with a pointed stake or pole

Manx. Relating to the people, customs, and area of the Isle of Man

Mesopotamia. The land along the Tigris and Euphrates Rivers, which is now modern Iraq, as well as some parts of northeastern Syria, southeastern Turkey, and southwestern Iran. Known as the "cradle of civilization," because it was here that the first agricultural communities and urban centers arose

miniseries. A television program presented in several episodes

mortar. A sturdy bowl in which ingredients are pounded or rubbed with a pestle

novella. A work of fiction longer than a short story but shorter than a novel

penny dreadful. A novel, usually sold in series form and often of adventure or violence

pestle. A clublike utensil used with a mortar to grind ingredients together

psychic vampire. A vampire that does not drink its victim's blood but instead drives its victim mad

reanimate. To bring back to life something that was dead

Romany. A group of wandering peoples that first appeared in Europe at the beginning of the sixteenth century. Also called *Gypsy*

Scottish Highlands. The area of Scotland that includes the rugged, mountainous northern and western regions

shape-shifter. A creature that can change its shape

Slavic. Relating to the peoples of Eastern Europe who speak variants of the Indo-European language family, including Belarusian, Bulgarian, Czech, Polish, Serbian and Croatian, Slovene, Russian, and Ukrainian

slayer. One who kills vampires and other demons

suave. Something that seems sophisticated and gracious but in a superficial way

Sumer. Center of the ancient Sumerian empire (5300 BC–1940 BC) in Mesopotamia

supernatural. That which appears to ignore the laws of nature

tag line. A phrase used to advertise a movie or TV show

talon. The sharp, often curved, claw of an animal and especially of a bird of prey, such as an eagle or a hawk

tracker vampire. A vampire that stalks its prey with the intent to kill it

unkempt. Messy and uncared for

Walpurgis Night. A traditional religious holiday celebrated on April 30 to May 1 in Central and Northern Europe. It is thought that the divide between the living and dead is at its weakest on this night.

wolfsbane. A kind of plant, also called monkshood; said to repel vampires

Index

Credits

Abbreviations Used

iSP = *iStockphotos.com*; JI = *Jupiter Images*;
LoC = *Library of Congress*; PD = *Public Domain*;
PF = *Photofest*; SS = *Shutterstock*; Wi = *Wikimedia*

l = left, *r* = right, *t* = top, *b* = bottom; *m* = middle

3 SS/Margaret M. Stewart **4–5** JI **6***bl* PF **6***tr* JI **7***b* JI **7***r*
SS/Andreas Meyer **8–9** SS/LANBO **10***br* SS/Bliznetsov
11*m* Wi/PHGCOM **11***br* JI **11***tr* iSP/Ernest Warnielius
12*bl* Wi/PD/McLeod **13***tr* SS/Bliznetsov **13***br* Wi/Josu
Goñi Etxabe **14** Wi/Dante Gabriel Rossetti/PD **15***bm*
SS/Ralf Juergen Kraft **15***tr* JI **16–17** SS/Robert F.
Balazik **18***tl* SS/W. Holger **18***br* SS/Nikolay Titov
19*tl* SS/Olga OSA **20** SS/Sergey Galushko **22***lm*
Wi/PD **22***tr* Wi/PD **23***m* SS/ Sandro V. Maduell **23***m*
University of Texas **23***r* SS/Annamaria Szilagyi **24–25**
SS/Dumitrescu Ciprian-Florin **25***m* Wi/PD **25***br* Wi/
PD **26**lm Wi/PD **26***m* Wi/Dd1975 **26***br* Wi/Julian
Nitzsche **26***tr* SS/Florin Mihai **27***tl* Wi/Cristian Chirita
27*m* SS/Xalanx *27bl* emeryandsue.com **27***rm* JI **28***tl*
SS/Perrush **28***br* Wi/Josh Berglund **29** PF **30***bl* Wi/PD

30*tl* Wi/PD **31***l* PF **31***tr* PF **32**bm Wi/Chris Kirk **32**tm
Wi/PD **33***bl* SS/Ioan Nicolae **34–35** SS/Nicola Vernizzi
36 Wi/Joachim Jesußek **37***bm* SS/daseaford **37***r* SS/
Algol **38***tl* SS/Cathy Keifer **39***br* JI **39***tr* SS/Dmitry
Tereshchenko **40***lm* LoC **41***r* Wi/PD **42** Wi/Shawn
Allen **43** SS/Ronen **44***tl* Wi/PD **44***tr* SS/Wojciech
Wojcik **45***t* SS/Zelenenkyy Yuriy **46***bl* SS/Mircea
Bezergheanu **46***m* PhotoToGo/IndexOpen **46***tr* iSP/Phil
Jackson **47** JI **48–49** SS/Chris Harvey **50***bl* flickr/
webandthecity **50***rm* flickr/Anders B. **51***lm* LoC **51***bl*
Project Guttenberg/PD **51***br* PF **52***bl* PF **52***tr* PF **53***br*
PF **53***tr* PF **54***bl* PF **54***tr* PF **55***tl* PF **55***tr* PF **55***br* PF
55*bl* PF **56***tl* PF **56***bm* PF **56***tr* PF **57***tr* PF **57***br* PF
57*bl* PF **58***l* PF **58***m* PF **59***tl* PF **59***r* PF **60** PF **61***bl*
PF **61***tr* PF **62***lm* PF **62***m* PF **62***rm* PF **63***tl* PF **63***br*
PF **64***bl* SS/Sascha Burkard **64***tr* PF **65**tm SS/Virginia
Gossman **65***bl* PF **65***tr* Wi/Bernd Haynold **66***bl* PF **66***br*
PF **67***bl* PF **67***tr* PF

Backgrounds JI; SS/Albo003

Cover SS/Margaret M Stewart; SS/ Andrey Ushakov;
Jesper Jurcenoks; JI; Wi/PD; JI